HUMP DRIVERS

HUMP DRIVERS

AN AMERICAN PILOT'S ACCOUNT OF FLYING OVER THE HIMALAYAS DURING WWII

ARTHUR LA VOVE

Library of Congress Control Number: 2020943538

Cover design by Jack Chappell
Type set in Hanseif/Montserrat/Heuristica
scene of sunset on Mountain Peaks "panchachuli" In Indian Himalaya © Dchauy. Courtesy of www.shutterstock.com

ISBN: 978-0-7643-6166-1
Printed in India

Published by Schiffer Publishing, Ltd.
4880 Lower Valley Road
Atglen, PA 19310
Phone: (610) 593-1777; Fax: (610) 593-2002
E-mail: Info@schifferbooks.com
Web: www.schifferbooks.com

CONTENTS

FOREWORD

This book was written by our father, Arthur La Vove, over the course of 1945–46, to accompany detailed drawings of his experience as a "Hump Driver"—a pilot—flying cargo and troop transport planes over the Himalayas mountain range between China, Burma, and India toward the end of World War II.

Arthur La Vove, circa 1947

The manuscript was written in discrete sections corresponding to particular illustrations: drawings and text were affixed accordingly.

This is a deeply personal account of one man's firsthand observations and experiences of an all-too-often underreported and underappreciated theater of World War II. *Hump Drivers* was created and written in 1945–46 by our father shortly after his return to the United States: the drawings and text are as they were drawn and written seventy years ago.

Upon reading *Hump Drivers,* the reader will feel that he or she has encountered a document from a "time capsule."

As such, the editors believe *Hump Drivers* is an important historical document. The text and drawings are presented as originally as possible, with a minimum of editorial intervention.

As to the actual drawing "paper": our father used paper that was available to him at the time he observed the action and drew the images. The narrative text was written to support and explain the depicted scenarios.

Our thanks go to Mary Ann Spinelli, who photographed the drawings. Mary Ann's father was also a World War II veteran: Sgt. Gabriel Spinelli, United States Army—China-Burma-India (CBI) theater of operations.

The publication of this book is especially timely, since China and India, indeed all of Asia, have gained considerable political, economic, and cultural importance worldwide: this story tells the reader about a pivotal time in this region's history.

We wish to dedicate our appreciation to our family and friends for their constancy and active support for this project since its inception.

Timothy La Vove
Michael La Vove
Susan La Vove Curley

INTRODUCTION

THIS IS about Americans who, during World War II, drove overloaded transport airplanes for the US Army's ATC over a foreboding stretch of terrain called the Hump, which looms between Assam, India, and China.

It used to be that flying was romantic. Pilots were regarded as glamorous super beings, aerial knights armored cap-a-pie in boots, breeches, scarves, leather jackets, and begoggled helmets. Their chargers were the flimsy, treacherous kites of WWI. The fliers I knew were not glamorous at all. They rarely called themselves pilots. Instead they referred to themselves as airplane drivers; hence the term "Hump Drivers."

They were either slender, smooth-cheeked, homesick, army-trained kids or elderly, weary Service pilots who, before the war, had flown as hobbyists or commercially. They were alike in that they had little food of poor quality, they worried about insufficient aircraft maintenance, they had no adequate weather-reporting facilities, and "communications" were a laugh. They were engaged in a mission supplying nonfighting armies for which they had no heart and that evoked an immense cynicism. They bucked not only weather and gigantic mountain ranges but frequently the armed Japanese fighter as well—and these young-oldsters (armed with .45 pistols!) flew defenseless, lumbering aerial trucks.

Those Hump Drivers who were commissioned had rank, from flight officer on up to major. But basically they shared the same food and misery with the GI Hump Driver who, as mechanic, radio operator, and cargo loader, made that mighty, horrible, impudent thing known as the "Hump Operation" possible.

They were all told that the State Department had its reasons for the operation, and, of course, the military came forth with mumbo-jumbo called "operational exigencies." But these kids, young and old, felt and acted like truck drivers. They had a stretch of terrain to cross—some 500-odd miles.

There were mountains there—some of them more than 20,000 feet tall.

There was weather—the clinging, suffocating monsoon or else the horrible, black, high-altitude icy winds of winter that drove airplanes far off course until fuel ran out and men whispered hopefully to God and then parachuted into the unknown.

In Assam, these Drivers lived in flimsy basha. They ate K rations and Spam until heartburn forbade. They slept in suffocating, rot-infested beds and gasped while mosquito nets kept any relieving breath of air from reaching their clammy, reeking skins.

China, for them, meant danger-filled groping for a landing through overcasts that shrouded the inexorable, waiting mountains. It meant more filth, poorer food, and the whiplash of "turnaround" time.

"Unload and get going!" is a phrase that haunts hundreds of former Hump Drivers.

China also meant rat-infested hostels—rickety brick-and-plaster buildings; it meant sharp-faced, shrewd "allies" who stole avidly. It meant hours of lying in excrement-lined slit trenches while Japanese planes flew overhead and bombed. It meant taking off with marginal fuel for the headwinds to Assam, and the sticky, bamboo rot of the monsoon.

Once in a while the Japanese would pounce and claw, scattering the slow B-24 Liberators, Commandoes, and C-47s. The greatest enemy, however, was the Hump itself; the weather and the frenzied hurry, rush, and "get there and come back," which meant insufficient rest and poor maintenance. That was the killer.

Between Fort Hertz and the Salween River lie many of the young-old kids, officers, and enlisted men—pilots, radio operators, and crew chiefs. The jungles have probably claimed them. The crumpled masses of metal, instrument panels, engines, cargo, and bodies are as one with that ancient, eternal place that does not care about the Japanese, the Kuomintang, the Communists, or Russia—or the atom bomb.

This book does not intend to cast recrimination. The dead cannot return, save in sealed caskets. Instead, this is intended as a nostalgic "Say, remember when—" sort of thing. Now—years later, the weather and the Japs, the jungle with its heat and leeches: Calcutta with the pungent, eye-stinging smog of burning cow dung, Kunming with its smell of water buffalo urine, human excrement, and garlic-saturated cooking, all seem wistfully attractive—like the faint, responsive chord induced by music of some almost totally forgotten, adolescent thrill.

This book will merely try to affix, for time, how the "Hump Drivers" looked, how they lived—where they lived—and how the people of India and China seemed to them. Perhaps this will be more appreciated by the Drivers than "outsiders," because unless one has lived in an Indian bashie or Chinese hostel; unless one has "sweated out" the Hump; unless one has been driven almost to the point of insanity with longing for that faraway place called home; unless one has been a GI mechanic fumbling with frozen, awkward hands at an icy engine in far-off Hsian—or perspired rivers of sweat on a workstand beneath Assam's humid, blazing sun—how could one really appreciate these memories?

India is so old—horrible and beautiful at the same time. And China is so menacing, forlorn, and tragic. And these two vast lands with their peoples were so foreign to the poor, struggling, young-old Drivers who found themselves doing a dreary, thankless job and who did not like their job, but who nevertheless did it to the best of their ability—which was far superior to anything done by the Chinese, Indians, Japanese, British, and Burmese.

So, I dare say, it is actually for the Drivers that this book has been written—with pictures and text. It is stuff that, perhaps, the professional correspondents and specially assigned artists could not have brought back. After all, *they* were civilians: *they* could leave whenever they wished.

We could not. We were military. We were "under orders."

Arthur La Vove

#1
NEWCOMER

HUMP DRIVERS

NEWCOMER

A DRIVER, as a rule, was a youngster. It took his first trip, on the gauges, over the Hump, before he became an oldster. And after his twentieth—as first pilot—he generally became hardened and cynical about his superiors and mission beyond his years.

But as a newcomer to the CBI the Driver was a kid who had been very proud of his Wings and who had been subjected, all along the way to India, to a progressive series of shocks caused by the climate, filth, the natives, and the callousness of the Orient itself toward everyone and everything.

His adventures in flight training and subsequent travels throughout the States had been remarkable feats in themselves. He had grown accustomed to handling all sorts of airplanes, the finest officers' clubs were available for his enjoyment, and those flashing wings against a breast encased in dark blouse or fine, brown-green shirt had been a remarkable lure for Romance.

And he had been in the States. The language, whether slurred and drawled or sharp and clipped, was His and Understandable. And the cities and towns were clean and comfortable.

Even if 3,000 miles intervened between himself and his hometown, it was still the USA—but India was different.

He looked at rice paddies; the arid stretch of the Sind desert—the unfamiliar architecture of Karachi, Delhi, Calcutta; and finally the jungles and tea plantations of Assam, and he felt the lurking hostility of an ancient and remote land and civilization. He was repelled and nauseated by the sights and smells.

En route he had been chivvied and bullied and treated like excess baggage by harassed and disgusted GIs and officers who had developed an armor of quiet, unspoken hatred for India and everything that was in it.

"Where YOU goin', lootenant?"

"I'm supposed to go to a place called Chi-boo-ah."

"Lessee yer orders."

And then the GI who handled passengers on the Army airline that crossed India said: "Sorry. Yuh got a number three priority. You'll have to wait till there's room."

That had been his lot all across India. Wait—sweat out space in a bucket-seat transport. Sleep in transient-area tents and bashies. He made his acquaintance with dhobie itch, sweat, heat, and pilfering natives. An ornate restaurant in New Delhi caused him later to run with pain-racked bowels to a latrine in the base at Agra.

But finally he arrived in Chabua and was "processed" by Personnel and Operations and Billeting and assigned to quarters. Meanwhile his pulse had quickened. This was the threshold of the Hump. At transient messes all along the way he had heard tall, wild, chilling stories of the Hump. He had listened to conversation that was morbid and bloody, which made him wonder if he would ever see home again.

Now he had finally arrived. He had spent several nights at the Polo Ground billeting area, where night-prowling jackals had raised his hair with their strange most of screams that sounded like those of women being torn to pieces; he had eyed the slit trenches and the huge red ball that warned of air raids, and he wondered if the trench was deep and safe enough against bombs and machine-gun bullets.

Now the billeting clerk had assigned him quarters in a certain bashie in one of the areas. That would be his home for the time being. A slight Wog* with loins wrapped in a filthy gray dhoti† hoisted his baggage to his head and walked at his heels toward the bashie.

When he entered the dark, musty interior, he saw a number of men standing, sitting, and a few reclining on their charpoys. A hum of conversation died as he stood there and tried to look casual while his eyes widened and his sweat-beaded lips twitched.

The Drivers already there eyed his too-new, wilted bush jacket. They felt a little resentful. They had just received an issue of hot, canned PX beer. If this bastard thought he'd chisel in—

"I—I'm supposed to be assigned to a bunk here," finally said the newcomer.

One of the old tenants indicated a vacant bunk. It was wedged in the far corner. Moldy shoes, dust-covered flight gear, empty K-ration boxes, and cigaret butts littered the floor. "Take Forzinsky's bunk," he said.

The Wog started toward it and deposited the baggage. The newcomer followed and then gave the bearer a rupee. The latter touched his forehead, nodded toward his right shoulder, and padded away. In the center of the room the conversation was resumed. The veterans talked and joked and chuckled and opened their hot beer and profanely put their lips over the foaming geysers that jetted ceilingward.

The newcomer sat on the edge of the charpoy‡ and stared down at the floor. He could feel a warning tingle of heat rash creeping down his back.

It was so dirty and hot and strange, and he felt very much out of place and unwanted. Suddenly he thought far, far back to a winter day at home when he was a kid, and the rest of the gang admiringly stood while he prepared to belly-whop with his new, shining Flexible Flyer. And a lump came up in his stomach and he had to bite his lips hard.

"What's your name," said a voice. He looked up and saw an elderly, grayish, thin man—quite nude, looking down at him.

"Anderson," he said slowly.

The older man grinned and extended his hand. "I'm Mullins. Welcome to the Ape's Nest. How about a beer—it's hot, but since all of us are only flight officers, looeys, and a coupla captains, we don't rate refrigerators like the colonels. Besides you'll get used to hot beer after a while."

Anderson held himself very steady. He said: "Thanks. I'd sure like a beer."

"Hey, you bastards," roared Mullins. "Let's welcome Andie here."

The others looked toward them and then slowly came toward Anderson's corner. A can was thrust into his hand, and then the questions came thick and fast. Where had he trained? Where was he from? How were things in the States?

And before he quite realized—after a few more beers—the bashie[§] was actually home, and he felt at ease and almost happy about it all—

* * * * * * * * * * *

WOG: According to military legend, this is an abbreviation of "Western Oriental Gentlemen." The story goes that a pompous British brigadier, alarmed by friction between English Tommies and Egyptians, convened his troops and in no uncertain terms gave them to understand that the natives were "western oriental gentlemen." The Tommies, similar in many respects to GIs, quickly shortened that description to the initials, i.e., Wogs. The phrase quickly spread from barrack to post, and by the time the Americans reached India, all natives of that unhappy land were known as Wogs. The Yanks themselves could never quite believe that the native of India was truly an Indian. He felt that a real Indian was indigenous only to the United States. So, without a sense of racial discrimination, he quickly seized on the term "Wogs." To the Driver, a Wog applied to any person born and raised in India, regardless of whether Hindu, Parsee, Ghurka, Sikh, or Moslem.

DHOTI: A linen garment, similar to a king-sized diaper worn by the majority of Indians

CHARPOY: A type of bed consisting of heavy linen bands secured to a wood frame. Durable but hardly comfortable.

BASHIE: Any type of dwelling or structure formed by bamboo pole uprights, chicken wire, and walls of whitewashed cheesecloth. The floors were usually poured cement, and the roofs were made of thatched bamboo.

#2
YOU SAY ONE TIME HOW MUCH

HUMP DRIVERS

YOU SAY ONE TIME HOW MUCH

THOSE WHO were stationed in China sometimes found romance.

One had to have a jeep, though. With a jeep almost anything could be accomplished.

The routine was down to earth. First there was the acquisition of a trip ticket from the jeep dispatcher. Armed with that, the MP's fangs were drawn.

A pair of army blankets were folded in the back seat and then one drove into Kunming, weaving in and out of ricksha and pedestrian traffic.

Jing Ballew Street was the trysting place. The technique was simple. When the jeep coasted to a stop, the tiny, flat-faced, eagerly whispering girls came forth like shadows. Their voices were throaty and their pidgin-English jarred on Occidental ears.

"Allo Joe—"

"Hiyah, babe."

A giggle. Then: "You lof me, Joe?"

"How much, babe?"

"Too t'ouzan' see-en."

"Boo-how, sugar—too guddam much. Ding boo-how."*

The shadows would move closer. Rice powder and the reek of garlic and human perspiration would reach forth.

"You say wan time 'ow moch!"

"Thousand see-en."

A shrill chorus of protest. "No, no, no-no-no-no!"

One shrugged, started the jeep, and shifted gears. Immediately: "O-chay, Joe—O-chay. Lozza go."

The shadowy forms slipped in, became substance—pliant bodies that were warm, that returned embrace for embrace—that had no inhibitions. And so the jeep joined the caravan of other vehicles that slipped out into the night and wandered toward the black hills.

Thus, out along the Burma Road—on the outskirts of Kunming—one tried, with Yuna wine and one of these giggling, sighing, passionate sparrows to get something before it was too late . . .

* * * * * * * * * *

* Ding How: "Pidgin' English for good. Ding boo-how—god-awful!

#3
COMMAND POST IN YUNNAN

US LIAISON TEAM
Command POST
IN YUNNAN - '44

COMMAND POST IN YUNNAN

SOMEONE SAID that the back area of China—the Yunnan Plateau—had known white men for a mere two or three generations. And the number of white men had been few.

But during the war, the Chinese had learned to know the lean, hard-bitten, dour-eyed US combat teams—officers and enlisted men, who lived in tiny villages; who ate, slept, and fought with Chinese—who risked disease, privation, and loneliness in order to try to shape coolies into trained, disciplined soldiers.

One could spot these "Megwas."* They were taciturn; many suffered from dysentery, jaundice, or dengue. They would appear in Kunming, get drunk, and raise hell on "Jing-Bow"‡ juice and then go back to the tiny villages whose ways and customs have not altered in a thousand years.

They had learned to fight the Japanese along the treacherous banks of the Salween. They knew how to use carbine, dynamite, and mortar in the bloody siege of Tengchung.

For these infantrymen, engineers, and artillerists, the tour of duty stretched on interminably. They had no operational rotation. They already could count twenty, thirty months of service in the theater—with no relief in sight.

They hated it, and, what was worse, they had given up hope of ever getting out. They had almost forgotten what Uncle Sugar† looked, felt, and smelt like—but they stuck to it and went on and on and on . . .

* * * * * * * * * *

* MEGWAS: Chinese for "Americans." At least the spelling is as close, phonetically, as the author can get.

† UNCLE SUGAR: During the war the Morse code alphabet was keyed by complete words for oral accuracy. A—able, B—baker, C—charley. Hence the US and/or USA was always and nostalgically referred to as Uncle Sugar or Uncle Sugar Able—a rich, benevolent, and frequently despotic and forgetful blood relation!

‡ JING-BOW JUICE: Jing-Bow is the phonetic spelling of "Air Raid" in Chinese. We called locally brewed alcoholic drinks, particularly Yunnan wine, "Jing-Bow" juice. The taste and aftereffects earned the description.

#4
INTERROGATION (MYITKYINA)

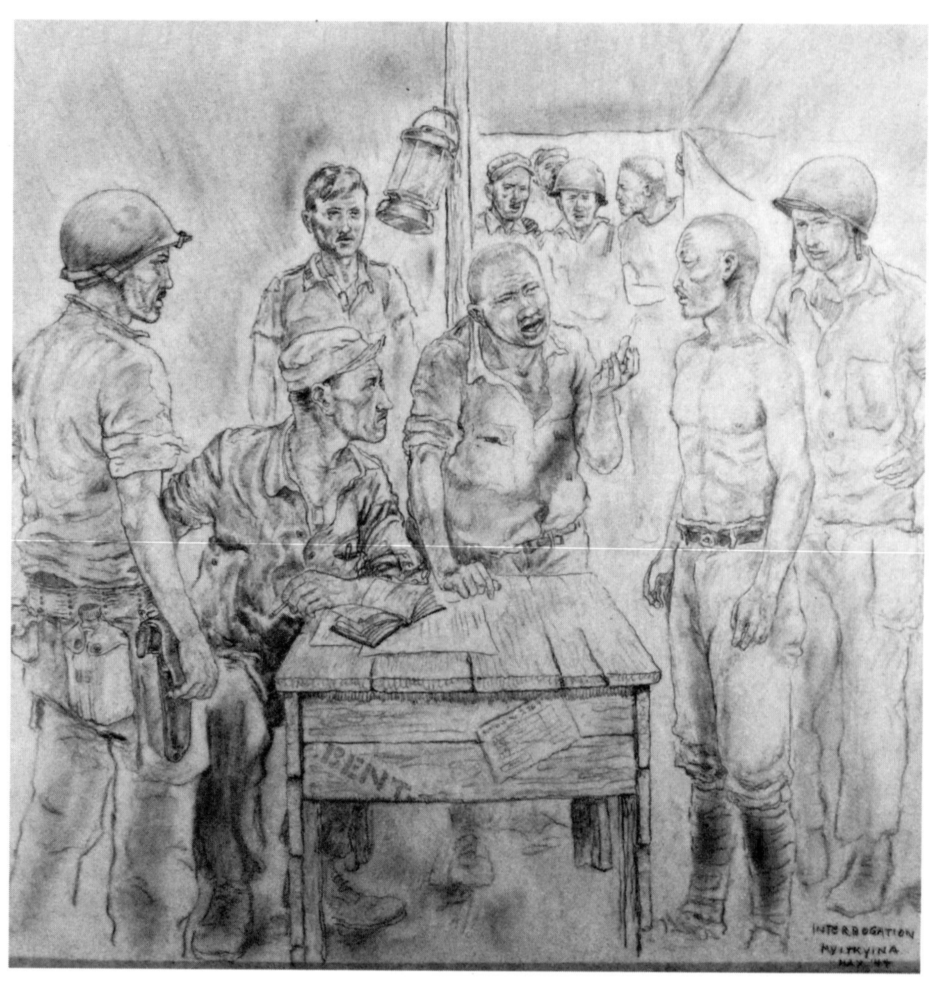
INTERROGATION
MYITKYINA
MAY '44

INTERROGATION (MYITKYINA)

THEY CALLED them "Merrill's Marauders." Officially, the Brass Hats in New Delhi referred to the organization as the "Galahad Force."

They were a collection of roughnecks who had volunteered for a special, particularly dirty type of assignment: Jap killing in the Burma jungle.

Before they left the vicinity of Bombay, where they had received a certain amount of additional training, both the British and the Wogs wondered if it had been wise to call Americans into the CBI.

They beat up military police, got drunk, and broke bottles, windows, and heads with cheerful indiscrimination. They struggled through several hundred horrible jungle miles and threw the Japanese out of Myitkyina in Burma.

Hump Drivers ordinarily never met real, fighting American soldiers. But during the hectic days of May, June, and July of '44, the Hump Drivers shuttled in and out of Myitkyina in Burma. They brought supplies to the Marauders and evacuated wounded to the receiving hospitals of Assam Valley.

The Drivers—pilots, crew chiefs, and radio operators—always used to carry extras—magazines, cigarets, candy, and, sometimes, liquor gleaned from a source of supply that was practically nonexistent. But nothing was too good for the combat infantry. They had captured Myitkyina.* That meant the Jap pursuit 'planes were forced farther south and east. It meant that the Hump Drivers could now steer their wallowing 'planes over safer, more easterly courses that were not quite so high.

The Drivers were, themselves, bewhiskered, unkempt, and tired. Yet, the sight of these infantrymen, gaunt unto the point of death, came always as a shock.

- - - - - - - - - - -

* Pronounced Mish-shin-naw

And their odd, professional air under ground fire was a never-failing source of wonderment to the Drivers. Once, while a C-47 drooped by the runway with its props lolling like parched tongues, a sniper had opened fire. The Drivers stood and stared and gaped, just like pedestrians during a midafternoon downtown holdup. The Marauders dropped flat, wriggled here and there—looked carefully and then fired efficiently.

Once in a while they would catch a live Jap. And then everyone who could would crowd around and watch and listen and study the Jap while funny shivers went up and down spines.

The line officers were as dirty and tired as the rest. They would sit and glower while the interpreters—some of them Chinese, others Nisei—kept hammering and hammering at the Jap.

"Ask the sunovabitch what outfit he's with," said an officer.

The interpreter wet his lips and talked to the prisoner. The Jap, short and stocky, blinked and said nothing.

The officer wiped sweat from his eyes. Outside, distant automatic fire sounded like kids' firecrackers in another section of town.

"Tell 'im that we'll be good to him—y'know: good chow, beer, and all that stuff," said the officer.

A GI laughed hoarsely.

The interpreter tried again and then the Jap shuffled and began to make sounds—they sounded like squeaks.

"A guddam pansy," said someone.

As two onlooking Drivers turned away, they heard an infantryman say: "Why waste time—skin the sunuvabitch with a dull knife an' have done with it . . ."

#5
KUNMING OFFLOAD

KUNMING
OFF-LOAD

KUNMING OFFLOAD

WHEN THE Burma Road fell to the Japs, all the Chinese-operated trucks withdrew to the Yunnan Plateau. The Nationalist government needed help, and since air became the only route, the Hump had to be crossed.

A man named Colonel Jordan made a deal with Chiang Kai-shek wherein Chinese trucks, drivers, and coolies would contribute to the war effort by offloading Hump airplanes.

That was sometime late in 1942. When 1944 rolled around and Hump Traffic had increased some 5,000 percent, the battered, weary, decrepit, falling-apart trucks were still trying to take care of the mountains of cargo that poured in.

The Chinese coolies were hounded, pushed, bullied, and beaten into handling the drums of gas and oil, heavy aircraft engines, bombs, ration cases.

GIs supervised the starveling coolies. It was an ordeal for both. Occidental tempers flared at Oriental fumbling. Curses and blows were exchanged. Meanwhile the trucks slowly died. Many times, swarms of coolies had to push a truck to the airplane, unload the ship, and then push the truck off the field to where the cargo could be transferred to a warehouse.

Truck beds collapsed and coolies fell into the chassis. Often they emerged unhurt; sometimes they fell beneath the wheels. The Drivers despaired. The decrepit vehicles increased ground time. It was wasteful, inefficient, but it was the best that could be done.

When the weather was dry, the dust enveloped airplanes, trucks, and coolies alike. During the monsoon rains, the field turned into a quagmire of red, slippery mud that defied men and machines. But the airplanes, despite accident, constant breakdown, and fumbling on the part of sick and weary Chinese, were unloaded.

GIs worked eighteen and twenty hours a day. Youths became hollow-eyed, gaunt, bitter old men; hands were calloused and clothing wore as thin as tempers. Theirs was not a fighting contribution. It was drudgery—inhaling dust, cursing and kicking at coolies, striving to keep battered trucks in operation.

The Drivers knew how it was with them. They were not indifferent, as so many of the ground lads bitterly claimed them to be. Hell—the Drivers had troubles enough of their own!

It was all part of the Deal . . .

#6
SWEATING OUT THE '29S AT CHENGTU

OPERAT
SWEATING O
THE '29's AT
CHENGTU, CH

SWEATING OUT THE '29S AT CHENGTU

THE B-29s were an awful lot of airplane. There had been scads of rumors about them. Long before they appeared in the CBI, the average Hump Driver imagined them in terms of hugeness that resembled fifteenth-century mariners' descriptions of sea monsters.

The project for bringing the Twentieth Air Force's big babies had been whispered, hush-hush, and top-secret from the very beginning. It had been known variously as the "Matterhorn" and "Twilight" projects. No one, except possibly Tokyo Rose, the Japs, thousands and thousands of runway-building Chinese and Indian coolies, newspaper correspondents, and Air Force brass, knew exactly what was involved.

Hump Drivers, based in Jorhat and Tezpur in Lower Assam Valley, began to fly their C-87s, loaded with cement mixers, rock crushers, bombs, and gas to the new, 2-mile-long runways that had come into being at the bases that surrounded the ancient capitol of Chengtu.

Weather reports were spotty; there were no adequate radio range facilities, traffic was heavy, and the fields were poorly lighted for night operations. But the Drivers put their ships in and then the 29s came along.

When they finally did show up, they looked surprisingly small after all the wild talk. Their crews acted like prima donnas at first. They were positive that they were going to win the war all by themselves.

Weren't they going to bomb Japan from bases 'way back in the guts of China?

The '29 crews were cocky—at first. But as time wore on and accidents began to take their toll, the boys quieted down. And the Drivers soon learned that a B-29 operation was a spectacle that could turn marrow to ice water.

There were the takeoffs. The Drivers would gather and watch, with sweating palms, as the overloaded bombers slowly rose into the dismal overcast that always gave Chengtu a melancholy, tearful aspect.

Too often, bombers did not make it. Engine "bugs" hitherto undetected showed up—and bombers and crews went up in smoke and flame.

And when the big boys came back from a mission, it was just as bad. The B-29 landings were a spectacle that, perhaps, the Romans could have appreciated. The Drivers did not.

Afterward—when the bombers were on the ground—the Japanese showed up and Drivers huddled in slit trenches while the maddened Nips tried to pulverize the ships that were damaging their homeland.

But these raids—Jing Bows, they were called—weren't as bad as the accidents. It was tough, sweating out the B-29's return; tough to watch one, with one or more feathered props make a wavering turn and suddenly stall and spin in . . .

#7
BIRD-CAGE ALLEY

YANKS IN
"BIRD CAGE ALLEY"
HSIAN—

BIRD-CAGE ALLEY

THERE WAS not much to be done in Hsian. As far as Chinese cities went, it was fairly clean and the shops offered an amazing assortment of gadgets—many of them made in Germany or Japan—at stratospheric prices.

Of course there was the "Temple of Love"—a very dirty brothel on the outskirts toward the field. But a man got tired of that after a while. Besides, in order to play with a Chinese whore, one had to get pretty stinking, and it was hard to get drinking stuff in Hsian.

Walking down the streets and watching the Chinese, who always stopped whatever they were doing and watched right back with interest, was a pretty good way to kill time.

There were all sorts of bazaars and shops and crooked alleyways that smelled of rice and garlic and human fecal matter and perspiration all rolled up into one. There were alleys that specialized in ornate metal pipes and copperware and bird cages. And there were always the Chinese who stared and jabbered animatedly with grins or watched with dull, uninterested eyes, and there were swarms of kids with running noses and racking coughs and blemished skins who tagged along and chattered and acted very much like kids from New York or Duluth, Waco or Los Angeles.

The Yanks would walk along and try to act superior, tough, and indifferent. But they actually weren't, and a Chinese grin and nod would bring a quick grin and nod in return . . .

#8
GOING OUT (KUNMING, HOSTEL 6)

GOING OUT (KUNMING, HOSTEL 6)

THE POKER game was interminable. It was there when a Driver returned from a trip, and it still went on when he left.

Everyone knew that his turn to fly would come with the same certainty of death and taxes. But the comfort about it, generally, was to be able to sit and play cards, or read or gossip while the rain slanted down against the leaking windows of the Chinese hostel and someone ELSE had to go out.

The Drivers used to call it rolling the dice with death. And the lad who had to go out and fly loads of rice or Chinese troops or horses or eggs and gasoline from one Chinese field to another, hundreds of black miles away, did not get much sympathy from his buddies.

One consolation was that each trip represented so many MORE of precious operational hours acquired—hours that, when they accumulated to a magical total, meant that a Driver could go home on operational rotation.

The very best thing about those days and nights was to be lying in the sack—half asleep, with the humdrum poker conversation helping to maintain a nice, blissful doziness—with the rough GI blankets just warm enough while the Driver going out told the temporary stay-at-homes to "Blow it outta their ars-holes!"

#9
ATC PILOTS WATCHING THE "CIRCUS" AT CHENGKUNG

ATC PILOTS WATCHING
THE "CIRCUS" AT
CHENKUNG —

ATC PILOTS WATCHING THE "CIRCUS" AT CHENGKUNG

EVERY AFTERNOON the Fourteenth Air Force at Chengkung would go out on a sweep, and that meant that for at least an hour, transport landing and takeoff operations were suspended.

The Drivers used to stand on top of bomb-dispersal dumps and revetments and settle down for an interesting time. It was thrilling to watch the fighters, overladen with bombs and gas, start their breathtaking and dangerous takeoffs.

Sometimes Drivers gasped and clenched their fists and watched helplessly when a pea shooter got away from the pilot and wound up in flame, earth- and ear-shattering explosions.

But mostly it was an exhibition of skill and speed, and the sleek lines and roaring engines wars gave evidence to the weary Drivers that a war was really going on in China. The Fourteenth's war, anyway.

Elgin Rittenbury, a youthful, tow-headed major, was the Air Transport Command's CO at Chengkung, and thus all the Drivers called the fighter takeoff's Rittenbury's Circus.

"I wouldn't want to goose them babies with all that gas an' dynamite for nothin'," said one Driver watching a Mustang flash down the runway before an audience of parked transports.

"I'll stick to C-46s," said another.

"Hell, yes," said the first one. "I only had two months with my wife before I came to the CBI."

"You guys act as stodgy as the clunks you drive," said a third. "You KNOW you'd give your left nut to drive a fighter. Don't crap ME.'"

It was always a relief when the last one left the ground. Especially to Ritt, who used to sweat out every takeoff and landing. He usually waited until the pea shooters had formed into formation and then disappeared en route to their strafing mission. Then he would go back to his office and the waiting pile of caustic, insulting, critical correspondence from the colonel, who, by virtue of a West Point background, had assumed command of the China Wing.

Flying an overloaded pea shooter was a cinch compared to some things . . .

#10
WALKOUT

WALKOUT

THINGS HAPPENED that were bad. Especially at night. There was ice and strong, bitter winds that no one had considered; winds that forced airplanes far off course. And, of course, they would never let one have too much gasoline for the return trip from China to Assam. So when the Drivers got lost and weak radio signals were of no help and fuel finally ran out, there was just one thing to do—step on out and parachute to the jungle, or the mountains or whatever there lurked below.

Maybe luck would hold and the crew would land, all in one piece, and get together on ground that wasn't Jap territory. Of course the 'chutes would open and the jungle kits would have all the stuff that intelligence swore they contained: matches, insect repellent, first-aid supplies, and machetes for cutting through growth.

The natives were supposed to be friendly. At least that is what was always said in Briefing. But, just the same, hold on to your forty-fives.

On the ground the Drivers—who were lucky—could wade down streams, always hoping that they had bailed near Assam. Sometimes they were lucky and did not have to be in the jungle more than a very few days.

Others finally emerged, months later—emaciated, disease-racked, leech-bitten spectres. If a man was unlucky and broke a leg and found himself alone, it was really tough. Sometimes natives found them and buried them and brought back something that could be used for identification.

The instruction books were written gaily. They had clever little cartoons and cute, humorous directions that made the whole thing seem like a jolly, Crosby-Hope venture with Lamour about to step into view at any moment.

But there was nothing humorous to one Driver who came down and dangled, upside down in the dark, from the branches of a huge tree on which his 'chute had stuck.

Evidently he could not release himself. Anyway, the big ants had gotten to him. When he was found, it was obvious that he had used six shots of his .45 in an effort to part the shroud lines—the seventh shot he used to escape the ants.

And the dark, miserable nights—cowering in the jungle—feeling for blood-sucking leeches and struggling with a soul in fearful despair while overhead transports sailed back and forth, unmindful of what was going on below.

It was said that in eighteen months, more than 800 airplanes went down between India and China. At least 50 percent of the crews must have come out . . .

#11
WAITING FOR PEA SHOOTERS AT KUNMING

WAITING FOR
PEA-SHOOTE
KUNMING -

WAITING FOR PEA SHOOTERS AT KUNMING

THE TOWER called and told traffic to stand by until Fourteenth Air Force pea shooters had landed.

Topside, fat C-46s, ugly Liberators, and long, shining fifty-fours circled and circled while the bitchy Mustangs came tearing in for a landing.

On the ground, the Drivers sat in their cockpits and watched and waited. They were all impatient. The pea shooters were holding up the war. So said pilots and copilots, radio operators, and crew chiefs. And topside, other Drivers held their altitudes and stared down at the slowly revolving panorama of red earth, mountain, and lake and cussed their luck.

The Mustangs had to show off. Before the squatting, prop-revolving audience of transports, the pea shooters swooped down, screamed a bare 50 feet over the runway, and then zoomed up and away.

Here and there a transport's prop ceased revolving. Presently all the waiting airplanes became silent, and the Drivers sat and watched while the Fourteenth came on in.

Many of the Mustangs had jaunty, impudent designs on fuselage and tail. The landings were flashy—in true, cocky, fighter-pilot hotshot style. One landed badly and bumped once, twice, three times.

"Lookit that silly bastard," snorted a Driver.

The Mustang ground-looped and came to a dusty halt just off the runway. And then the waiting Drivers saw the ambulance race out.

"Must have got hurt," said a radio operator.

The Drivers now were quiet, and then the gravel-voice control tower came to life and ordered the transports to get going.

Engines snorted and turned over. Other transports came in for ponderous, exhausted landings—their temporary vigil of circling done for the time being.

The Drivers, in turn, who were to take off, lined up with the runway and eased throttles forward. And as they swept on down and began to lift, they caught a side glimpse of the ambulance and the knot of khaki figures around the Mustang and a stretcher and a supine figure.

It was just not done—saying things out loud about a guy's tough luck—but dozens, each silently and blasphemously, pleaded to God, fate, or whatever. All that mental suggestion should have helped because every Driver and crew chief and radio operator mentally begged and pleaded for a break for the guy—whoever he was . . .

#12
DELHI SNAKE CHARMER

Delhi
Snake-Ch

DELHI SNAKE CHARMER

REMEMBER THE "wop" organ grinder and his red-jacketed monkey back home? Funny, but it was a hot day—and I was dressed up in my Sunday churchgoing clothes and felt stiff and uncomfortable as the starched collar chaffed my neck and perspiration dripped down between my shoulder blades.

The music made a strange sound, and the monkey acted sort of dumb, now that I think of it, and I thought the little Italian was funny with his strange twitching face and tattered clothing and odd accent, but now I wonder if he didn't feel bad that day.

Anyway, standing in a broiling-hot courtyard in Delhi, I watched that ragged Indian with his reed pipe and wicker basket and the sleepy-looking cobra that swayed a little bit while awful sounds came from the pipe. And I remembered that remote Sunday when I was a kid, and the poor little Eytie's face twitched as he cranked the organ while the monkey chattered and hopped with darting frightening eyes.

I never dreamt then that some day I'd go to India and actually SEE a snake charmer, and yet, here I was, watching a snake charmer, and I felt lousy and bored and hot and tired. My buddy had a camera, and he got a couple of pictures. There were other Indians standing next to us, and they looked as bored as I guess we did. When it was over, the snake sort of wilted and collapsed back in the basket, and we gave the charmer a rupee and then wandered down to Queensway and the Picadilly downstairs bar.

And while we sat in the bar under a fan and drank a gin-and-squash, I felt depressed and irritated and wondered how we would ever fix things so that pain-filled "wops" wouldn't have to grind organs, and ragged Wogs would do something else for a living beside blow lousy noises and torture poor, dismal snakes . . .

#13
MOVING CHINESE TROOPS

MOVING CHINESE TROOPS

THE TOP-SECRET order said that we would move Chinese soldiers from Hsian, in north-central China, to a place called Chanyi.

The reason was that the Japs had apparently decided to move in on the Kunming area. The Chinese troops, who had been herded and collected in Hsian, would be taken to Chanyi—about 50 miles northeast of Kunming—where they would prepare to resist the threatened advance.

The orders had originated in India, and all the staffs—generals, colonels, majors, and captains representing ground forces; the air force; Chinese top-rankers—all had convened and smoked countless cigarets and argued and used up reams of paper and finally had figured out how many troops would move, how quickly they would move, and whether it would work.

The plan had a fancy name: "Alpha Project" it was called, and it meant that umpty-ump airplanes would be necessary with umpty-ump crews.

By the time it got down to the Driver, his was a simple problem: to get to Hsian in one piece, take on a load of Slopies,* and bring them back safely.

Hsian was bitterly cold and dry. A wind that came all the way from the Great Wall and Siberia howled down over the parched terrain surrounding the ancient walled city and the airport, incongruously modern, which Russians had originally built during the thirties.

When the Drivers landed and taxied beside the runway, they eyed half-completed buildings and hangars, which all bore the scars of Jap bullets and 20-millimeter shells, which the fighter boys already based there called "Tojo's Chop."†

The ground operation was easy. A handful of GIs, shivering in cotton field jackets (the brass hats would not approve an issue of warm flight clothing for nonrated, ground personnel), had silent, uneasy rows of soldiers standing by.

This was the cargo for the Drivers to bring to the Kunming areas. The Chinese soldiers were all small and slight. Their eyes were sore with trachoma, their noses dripped slime, and they constantly coughed.

Their clothing consisted of torn, cotton trousers and blue-gray quilted jackets. They carried rifles—some of them German-type Mausers, others of Russian origin. They were armed with long, weird-looking Mauser automatic pistols in ungainly wooden holsters that could be used as an extension, thus making a carbine out of the pistol.

The GIs ran around and counted off the Chinese; twenty to a 'plane.

"Now make sure that these bastards don't move around during the takeoff and landing," urged a nervous Driver. "Have somebody tell 'em."

"They've already been briefed," said one of the expediting GIs. "They'll behave."

"You hope," said the Driver with a worried expression.

There were two or three American colonels, elderly men who wore infantry or artillery insignia. They held clipboards, stamped their feet, and shivered beneath greatcoats.

"Who are the Wheels," asked a Driver. "What are they doing?"

"Beats hell out of me," said the operations officer, a pilot who had been grounded for this special duty. "They just count the number of Slopies assigned to a ship and make a note of the ship's number."

"But isn't that what the GIs are doing?"

"Yeh."

"How come colonels are doin' it, too?"

"Beats me."

MOVING CHINESE TROOPS

Hurry, hurry, because of the urgency, the cold, and the lack of rest facilities. The Chinese were bundled into the airplane, and the tight-lipped crews took last, hasty drags at their cigarets before entering their cockpits.

You see, there were not enough parachutes for the passengers. But the Japs were advancing, and the rumor had it that Chiang was determined to have these troops moved. If an airplane went down—there were plenty more Chinese available. Let the crew (who all had 'chutes) bail out, and to hell with the passengers.

The Chinese sprawled on the cold, hard metal floors of the airplanes. When the crews tramped by them on the way forward to the cockpit, the soldiers looked up with half-friendly, half-scared eyes.

The great, iron bird repelled them. Bullets, hunger, disease, and dirt they could understand. But the noise of the engines and the vibration brought out all of their superstitious dread.

The crew chief usually stood in the cockpit doorway and watched during the takeoff. If any of the Chinese moved, he would shout at them. Maybe his gestures and yelling would hold them in their places. Maybe he would have to wave his .45 automatic and frighten them.

But they generally sat and stared like dark-eyed, frightened children, while the airplane gathered speed and slowly climbed for altitude.

"Stinking, no-good, goddamn Slopie bastards," muttered the pilot. "Watch. It'll get rough and they'll puke and piss and crap up the ship till hell won't have it."

The Drivers sat and stared at their instruments. And in their minds ran the dreaded thought. Suppose they had to bail. Would they be able to walk through the cabin and jump? Those Chinese were armed. Even a Slopie would get the message—figure that the Megwas were scramming. Maybe they'd have to shoot their way out of the ship.

But even if they COULD bail, would they? The crew chief came forward, his face screwed up in disgust. "Christ," he gasped, reaching for his oxygen mask. "The floor is covered with puke."

It made the Drivers so mad they felt like killing those Chinks. Getting the ships so messed up. But each Driver knew that he would never bail and leave his passengers. Hell—even if they were dirty and stinking, even if they DID steal when they could—they were human beings, weren't they?

"I could never bail and let those poor bastards go down," once said a kid—Gregory his name was. He was twenty-four and handsome.

He was a major and a base commanding officer. And he flew his share of Slopie trips along with the Drivers under his command.

"No," said Greg. "I couldn't ditch a load. After all—I'd have to live with myself afterwards, wouldn't I?"

One night the weather was hellish. Radio aids failed, ferocious winds aloft, hitherto unreported, were present, and there was ice in the overcast. The boys down below tried to keep contact with Greg up until the last minute.

When they found him months later, Greg had kept his promise—he and his passengers were together . . .

- - - - - - - - - - - -

* SLOPIES: A mysterious descriptive word used by "Megwas" to describe Chinese. The opinion of the troops was divided between two theories:

1. That all Chinese foreheads slope back

2. That the entire Chinese physiology has a tendency to "teeter-totter"

The author does not hold with either theory. He merely reports the fact that to Yanks, the Chinese were "slopies"—and that's that!

† TOJO'S CHOP: A chop is a seal carved of stone or ivory. The seal may be a personal name or the name of a government, business firm, or society.

MOVING
Chines
TROOPS

#14
SWEATING OUT 'PLANES IN ASSAM

Sweating out
Planes in
Assam!

SWEATING OUT 'PLANES IN ASSAM

IT WAS easier when a Driver was young. The older boys, Snake* pilots who were fat and fortyish, they were hard hit by the routine.

And it was a killing sort of grind. A Driver came back to his base after a rugged trip to find out that he was up on the pilots' list: that he had barely twelve hours in which to eat, relax, sleep, and take off again for China.

When the weapons-carrier driver woke one up, it was like struggling through fathoms of bad, black water.

"Transportation, sir," invariably said the voice behind the flashlight that burned through one's eyes.

Even if the monsoon heat was present, one shivered a little, groping in the dark for soggy clothing. But the worst blow of all was waiting for an airplane.

Some little thing had gone wrong. Maintenance was attending to it. So the Drivers sat and sat and sat while the mechanics worked in the dark rain and the hours dragged slowly by.

A few read. Others mechanically dabbed at solitaire. Some curled up on the hard benches in the "lounge." Mostly one sat and eyes got more leaden and waves of nostalgia and self-pity mounted and eddied. Finally—

"Lieutenant Jones?"

A head jerked up.

"Your ship's ready."

The officer straightened up painfully, stretched, and looked at his watch. He had been sweating it out for six hours. It was almost four in the morning. His copilot roused the radio operator and crew chief while Jones stiffly went back to operations to see if he would have to make out a new flight plan.

Once at the ship itself, the imminence of the takeoff woke everyone up. The whining noise of the putt-putt generating power in the

C-46's fat throat; the preflight inspection—all these things drove thoughts out of one's mind.

And the tightness of spirit continued and mounted through the disciplined anxiety of starting the engines; calling the tower, taxiing to the end of the runway, reading the checklist, running up the power. And, of course, there was the takeoff; tired eyes forced to harsh sharpness as throttles were advanced and 24 tons of metal hurtled through the rain down the bumpy runway.

Afterward, when the ship was safely off the ground and trimmed for climb, the Drivers could relax and ponder.

"Six hours sweating this crapper out. 'Least nine hours of flying, figuring we'll be on the gauges most of the time. Christ—we won't be able to hit the sack till God knows when . . ."

The copilot nodded and the radio operator and crew chief looked at one another. Jones was over forty—a service pilot. He should have been home with his wife and kids. He was awfully tired, but he had to go through with it. His copilot was twenty—and army trained. Jones didn't know that his copilot was also tired.

"Jesus. I can't cave in," thought the copilot. "Not in front of old man Jones—a dam' snake pilot, at that . . ."

- - - - - - - -

* SNAKE PILOTS: "Service" pilots. The wings worn by these people were distinguished by the letter "S" set against the shield in the center. The idea (it said in fine print) was that "Service" pilots were not supposed to go near combat zones. Army-trained pilots scathingly referred

to Service pilots (who got their training in civilian life before the war) as "Snakes." The latter's comeback was to call army- and navy-trained pilots "Government Wards."

#15
CHINA SIDE OPERATIONS

NOTICES
China Side Operations

CHINA SIDE OPERATIONS

IT WAS high on the Yunnan Plateau—and generally cold. During the monsoon, the rains came down cold and clothing was damp and leather equipment sweat moisture and stank.

The Drivers came into operations and huddled, grateful for a moment of imagined security—away from the darkness, the ice, the leaking cockpits, turbulent air, failing instruments. For precious minutes they were alive, secure, in a place of light, gossip. The return to India was a few hours away in their inscrutable future.

The brackish coffee lay warm in their stomachs, and the taste of the inevitable eggs was good. Some liked to sit quietly and read. Others loved to needle the operations officer.

A few argued quietly, intelligently, for more fuel with which to make the return trip. There were those who had imaginary mechanical ailments and who pleaded earnestly for permission to remain overnight. Some, when brusquely turned down, viciously damned the operations officer: damned ALL operations officers.

"So, I'm a sonuvabitch," he said. "All right, I'm a heel. I'm no good. But I don't run this lousy rat race. Tell Tom Hardin, why doncha. Now get your clearance and scram."

There were many who were impatient. They cursed the clumsiness of exhausted cargo-unloading supervisors and the fumbling efforts of three-fourths-starved, disease-racked coolie soldiers who drained the airplanes of gas drums, ammunition eases, and boxes of rations.

"Another pig-gutted hour ground delay for YOU, brother," snapped a smooth-cheeked, hollow-eyed flight officer.

"Quit bein' eager," said the operations officer. "An' watch your step. See these two bars on my collar. I'm a captain."

"Aw blow it," said the FO. "I'm gonna write THIS trip delay up but good. Why this lousy base has its head up an' locked. I get off my ship an' no truck, no Slopies, no nothin'. Not even a follow-me jeep."

"Soak your head," muttered the captain. "You got C-87 number 800?"

"Yeh."

"Then get goin'. It's been ready twenty minutes ago."

A quiet driver looked up from a tattered copy of Superman Comics.

"He wants to win the war," he said. He's all for Shanker Jack. He's also eager for the DFC."

The FO glared. The operations officer stood with his behind to the smoking store. "Shove off—into the wild blue, sonny. And give my regards to Black Bob."

A few bystanders guffawed. The door opened, bringing in cold and rain and wet newcomers. An airplane grumbled in the distance. The FO and his copilot melted into the darkness, and the operations officer lit another cigaret and decided not to think about the rough trip the kids were going to have on their way back to Jorhat. With one of those stinkin' C-87s, too—his hands trembled for a moment. It would be easy to blow his top—tell them Down There what they could do with the whole deal—

He sighed and straightened up. The colonel, big and important and with gleaming eagles on the shoulders of the newfangled green flying jacket, had just come in.

"Good evening, sir." Tone low, deferential.

"Evening." The colonel's gaze was frosty. In those eyes lurked no friendship. Drivers looked away. The background hum of conversation ceased. Men cleared their throats, studied weather reports; scribbled on Form 23s.

Two Drivers watched the captain, so rigid behind the counter.

"Lookit the brown-nosing sunovabitch," whispered one.

#16
SHOPPING IN DIBRUGARH

RARE
JEWELS

SHOPPING IN DIBRUGARH

IT WAS just about 18 miles along a dusty, rutted road Northeastward from Chabua. On off days or nights, Drivers and paddlefeet alike could either jeep it; crowd onto jolting, swaying six-bys; or else thumb hitches from the slow, middle-of-the-road British convoys.

The goal was the little town of Dibrugarh, a collection of back alleys, tea planters' stilted houses, a railroad terminal, and the bazaar where everything and anything could be bought.

On Wednesday and Saturday evenings, officers could go to the dances at the Tea Planters' Club—a barnlike place where brown-skinned bearers served tepid gin and squash highballs. A handful of pallid tea-plantation women—wives, daughters, nieces of English functionaries, a few American army nurses or Red Cross girls and, sometimes, English and Anglo-Indian or Burmese "Sisters"—were available for dancing to the tunes coming from scratchy records.

But the main thing was the shopping—for Lily Brand gin, Bull Fighter–type brandy, and souvenirs. The bazaar was a labyrinth of knick-knacks and smells. Here the fulsome aroma of perspiration combined with garlic and burnt cow dung made India real with stunning impact. A visit to the bazaar was always deadening, but the folks at home wanted souvenirs. And so the Drivers came to search, haggle, and argue over the thousands of decorated velvet purses, hand-carved brassware, ivory figurines, cheaply put-together silver, and gold-plated jewelry and imitation gems.

Every shopkeeper had the same pleading, shrinking smile. Every dealer's name seemed to be Mukerjee. And each stall had its attending swarm of begging, emaciated, red-eyed, precocious children with pipe-stem limbs and puffed little bellies.

The best buy, of course, was in brassware. The trays and cocktail shakers, tumblers, and slim-necked decanters were, after all, obviously handwrought, definitely authentic Mother India.

"Kitna?"* said the GI, pointing to a decanter.

"Baksheesh,"† whined a little begger tugging at his arm.

The GI shrugged him off. "Kitna," he demanded again.

Mr. Mukerjee grinned with all his discolored teeth and stared raptly at the decanter as though its beauty and value had suddenly and amazingly become apparent.

"Thirty ruPEES, sahhb."

The GI scowled. "Too dam' much. Piss poor, Joe."

Mr. Mukerjee hunched his shoulders and seemed to visibly shrink in height. "You rich man, sahhb. Thirrty ruPEES not enough. This fine thing. Handmade, sahhb. Look." His thin, tapering fingers lovingly brushed over the handle.

"Huh. I seen one of these for ten roops down in Calcutta."

Mukerjee straightened, closed his eyes, and shook his head. "No," he said.

"Whaddya mean, no. I SEEN it, I tell yuh!"

The tiny begger returned and tugged again. "Baksheesh, sahhb. Me poor sick bassard! No momma, no poppa, no Uncle Sam, no per diem. Baksheesh, sahhb."

The GI slapped negligently, as though at a fly. "For ten roops in Calcutta," he repeated.

Mukerjee sighed. "I poor man, sahhb. Look. I show you receipt. Twenty-eight ruPEES I pay. Not possible to sell for less. I hav wife, children."

"Blow it," said the other GI.

"Baksheesh—bakshees."

"Scram, guddamit," roared the first GI.

The tot danced away, his wizened little face tight. "You sun uv beetch. You bassard. You big goddam." He spat and disappeared between two stalls.

The two Americans started away. Already four other Mukerjees darted forward, each brandishing ivory earrings and brassware. The first Mukerjee grasped the shopper's arm. "All right. Twenty-FIVE rePEES."

"Nuts."

"But sahhb. That is as low as I can go."

"Stick it."

Mukerjee's features twitched. His lips crumbled into an uneasy smile. "How much you offer?"

The GI's wiped perspiration from their foreheads. "Fifteen roops and that's it."

Mukerjee hesitated, closed his eyes, bit his lips, communed with himself. Then his shoulders drooped. He made a quick, birdlike nod. "Teak,‡ sahhb. Fifteen ruPEES."

The other Mukerjees turned away in disappointment, and the two Americans grinned at one another in triumph as Mr. Mukerjee began to wrap the decanter, which had, originally, cost him less than five rupees . . .

- - - - - - - - -

* KITNA: How much? (Hindustani)

† BAKSHEESH: Alms—used by beggars young and old throughout the Middle East and India

‡ TEAK: Short for tee-kie or "Okay" in Hindustani.

#17
A NIGHT AT ROGER QUEEN

A NIGHT AT
"Roger Queen"
(Kunming approach

A NIGHT AT ROGER QUEEN

THE HUMP Drivers knew Kunming Approach Control as "Roger Queen."

That was the system by which airplanes entering the China area could be diverted because of weather or special cargo to certain, specific fields.

Kunming Approach Control also had Traffic Control. The latter had the task of seeing to it that during bad weather, airplanes, circling for landings, were given specific altitudes that would prevent aerial collisions.

Despite that, however, collisions did happen because the men—officers and enlisted men—who worked in Traffic and Approach Control were only human, and a bare two years before all this took place they had been college or high school students, businessmen, or plain working people.

More than five hundred airplanes landed and took off from the Kunming Area within a twenty-four-hour period. Radio ranges were not always dependable and failed constantly. The weather was frequently vicious, and mountains jostled each field.

It was a task that would have staggered any professional who had worked for the US airways during peacetime. But the kids who manned Roger Queen took it on the chin and performed miracles. Despite the lack of facilities, inexperience of weather, and treacherous terrain, only a very few planes collided

Most of the officers who worked at Roger Queen were pilots themselves. For them the agonized, frenzied activity of a stormy night was worse than it was for the sweating, anxious Driver who sat upstairs and waited, at 18,000 feet, while ice formed and the fuel tank needles kept dropping toward zero.

The enlisted men who manned the microphones and telephones, who kept up the boards with cards that carried Estimated Times of Arrivals, checked reports and clearances—they sweated it out too.

It was funny how the voices of Drivers could tell what was happening. When a pilot called in and he deliberately kept his voice slow and steady, one could detect that faint humming that showed how tense and scared he really was.

Sometimes a Driver would call in frantically for help—a radio "fix." He wanted Roger Queen—and other stations to shoot bearings on him: tell him where he was. It was during those times when officers and GIs would sit over their huge maps and plot courses and estimate the amount of fuel the Driver had and how far he could go before running out.

When the time came, on bad nights, for shift changes, the old shift would linger and try to be helpful and wait nervously while the new shift took up the task of bringing in the lost ones.

"We haven't had a peep out of Niner-six-six-niner for the last twenty minutes," croaked a tired, blinking captain as he pulled on his flight jacket. "The plot I got I figure he must be somewhere between here and Paoshan."

The lieutenant who relieved him nodded and noted the entries and said nothing.

"If you work him in, lemme know, will yuh? I'll be down in my sack."

The captain hesitated while the sergeant who was going to drive him down to his quarters at Hostel 6 waited.

"Tell yuh what," said the captain. "I'll call you back in half 'nour."

"Roger," said the lieutenant. He did not look up at the other. Both he and the captain knew C-47 Niner-six-six-niner. It was a Kunming airplane. They knew the guys who were flying it.

The cigaret smoke got thicker and the phones jingled while officers and enlisted men stumbled from instruments to the boards to the maps and back to the instruments. Outside they could hear the steady droning of airplanes circling in the overcast while the rain kept drumming down.

At Hostel 6 the captain didn't feel much like sleeping. Instead he sat in on the poker game that had been going when he went to work ten hours before and was still going on.

In the enlisted men's area, the sergeant did not feel like sleeping either. He sat and tried to read "Strange Woman," but his ears kept hearing those airplanes.

The telephone at the CQ's office, just across from the captain's hostel, rang. A private answered and listened. Then he got up, put on his slicker, and slithered through the mud toward the officer's quarters. When the captain came out, the soldier said: "Got a call for you, sir. That ship made it okay."

"Thanks, feller." The captain rubbed his nose. "Jeez—thanks a million."

He walked back and slammed the man sitting next to him on the shoulders.

"What the hell's the matter with you," he yelled.

"Let's settle down an' play some real poker, f'r krissakes."

"Listen to him," snorted the other. "You act like you got orders sendin' you home."

"Naw—I just feel good. That's all."

He still felt good, even when the hand dealt to him only had a pair of lousy treys . . .

#18
BURMA ADVANCE

Burma
Advance
LAVOVE

BURMA ADVANCE

WHILE THE Drivers pounded against the dark winds that swept over the Hump's icy peaks, a column of Americans, below, were cutting their way through the Burma jungle.

Technically this gang was known as the Galahad Force, commanded by Brigadier Frank D. Merrill, a West Pointer. Later on, a bunch of war correspondents called the men Merrill's Marauders, thereby pleasing the general and giving the "Marauders" a type of mental heartburn that still seems to irritate its victims.

These were the experienced men of Guadalcanal, Port Moresby, and special training in jungles surrounding Panama. They had volunteered for a "special mission," and the lure had been this: do a good, dangerous job and, maybe, you'll get to go home.

They volunteered. They were tough. During their training days, hard by brass-ridden Bombay, they acted like the worst kind of dead-end kids.

It is hard for those who stayed at home to realize just how rugged these boys were—and perhaps still are. Many of them had already been in battle with the Jap. Others were equally as case-hardened: mentally, most of them decided that they probably never would survive the special mission.

The Marauders went to a jump-off place in Assam and, as far as the Drivers were concerned, totally disappeared. The first inkling that any of the Humpsters had of the whereabouts of this star-spangled bunch of adventurers was when they emerged, full of leech bites, malaria, dysentery, jungle rot, and a demoniac hatred of Japs and the Orient, to capture the main air strip near a town spelled Myitkyina and pronounced Mish-in-aw.

They had struggled, sweated, suffered, and died through several hundred miles of sheer hell; they had proceeded by stealth and battled like old-time Indians; they had bushwacked Japs and, in turn, had been bushwacked.

The capture of Myitkyina meant two things: it made possible the eventual reopening of the Burma Road, and it enabled the Drivers to fly lower and safer altitudes.

The Drivers stood in awe of the Marauders. It was bad enough being a foot soldier in the first place. But to be a doughfoot and have to walk and fight Japs hand to hand in the middle of a jungle! My God!

The Marauders seemed to like the Drivers. Perhaps it was because the kids brought in supplies and flew out the wounded and sick. But, perhaps, the greatest thrill that was ever experienced by a pair of Drivers happened one day when a Marauder—stripped to the waist, bearded, and sweating—bummed a cigaret, looked coolly at the C-47 that towered in the background, and said:

"How many machine guns do you guys carry in this clunk?"

The pilot and radio operator looked at each other, and then the pilot said: "You kidding!"

"No."

The radio operator, who was embarrassed because his clothes were comparatively clean and his cheeks were very smooth, said: "We don't carry no guns 'cepting these piss-poor forty-fives."

The infantryman gestured with his thumb. "Mean to say yuh fly where them Japs are without no machine guns. Just forty-fives?"

"Yeh."

The foot soldier's eyes widened a trifle. "Sa-ay," he said. He took another drag at the cigaret. "Jeez—kind of rugged, ain't it?"

The pilot stared at the man's sunburned shoulders and thought of the jungle and shuddered. "It's a little rugged," he said.

"Not for me," said the Marauder. "Fly without guns with those skibbies poppin' at me. I should say not—"

It was a funny war . . .

#19
KUNMING PASSENGER TERMINAL

NO
EXIT
ATC SCHEDULES
ARRIVALS
DEPARTURES

KUNMING PASSENGER TERMINAL

TOWARD THE middle of 1945, a slate-gray, plaster building with a red-tiled roof, sagging walls, and broken ceiling handled almost a thousand passengers a day.

The building measured 20 feet by 40 or 50. Along one side was an unvarnished counter constructed out of lumber that had originally been flown to Kunming in the form of packing crates and boxes.

It was here where orders were scanned by GIs and officers, and where air passage was issued or canceled. The military of America, China, Free France, and Britain and India mingled with civilian refugees from French Indo-China and missionaries from the interior of China.

Drivers tramped in and out, looking moodily at the human cargo they would carry to other fields of China or else back to India.

There were GIs and officers, all of them eager and burning-eyed with anxiety. They were the lucky ones who were going home. They besieged the desperate men who worked as ticket agents, who had to compile manifests and supervise the loading and unloading of airplanes.

Outside, the rains usually made the Kunming mud a slippery, treacherous sea through which navigated six-by-sixes and battered weapons carriers and jeeps. Inside, the air was fouled with the odor of unwashed bodies, stale tobacco smoke, sweat, and gun oil and leather.

Chinese baggage coolies plodded through the crowd, stepping gingerly over the recumbent forms of those who curled up on the floor and slept through the incessant din.

In a corner, a harassed officer "briefed" a group of passengers who were about to fly back to India in a C-54:

"The captain of the airplane is in full command," said the officer. His voice was hoarse. He had been saying this for months on end. "Although the trip is perfectly safe—we've flown the Hump for years—you have been provided with parachutes. On each 'chute is a jungle kit. The jungle kit contains items that will aid you in walking out to safety—"

The crowd followed his arm as he pointed out the items that were displayed on a board. "Here is the pocket compass, and here is a machete with which to cut your way through jungle growth, and here is a first-aid kit, and here—"

A GI, bitter after having waited two days, edged up to the sergeant at the counter: "For thirty-four stinkin' months I bin in China," said the GI. "Now when I got orders to go home, I gotta sit an' wait an' sweat out a ride."

"I told you," said the sergeant, "that high-priority passengers move first. There's still a backlog of twos an' threes. You got a four priority."

"You'd think," said the GI to a Driver, a lieutenant, who leaned on the counter, "that they'd give a guy a high priority after he'd had it, wouldn'tcha!"

"They got their heads up an' locked," said the Driver. "Lookit me. I got my time in an' I'm supposed to go home too. But I got a number four too."

The sergeant held a manifest in a hand that shook slightly. He had been going exactly fourteen hours straight, and he was afraid of crumbling to pieces. "It won't be long," he said. "Maybe this afternoon—"

In the corner, on a bench next to the dusty window, a thin woman—about thirty and almost pretty with her dark-blue eyes, quietly spoke to a little girl in French. A major and a private first class stood by and admired.

"She looks nice—just like an American girl," said the major.

"Wish I knew French," said the PFC.

"They're refugees from a place called Szemao—that's down in the southeast."

"Maybe the kid's hungry," ventured the PFC.

The major pursed his lips. He felt in the pocket of his frayed combat jacket. There was a bar of Nestle's tropical chocolate there, and he hesitated. He had been with the Marauders, and after coming to Kunming he had gained his promotion, but his habit of hoarding for emergencies was still strong. "Yuh 'spose the kid would go for this?" he asked the PFC.

"It's candy, ain't it," said the GI. "All kids like candy."

The major bent toward the woman and held out the bar. "Bon jour," he stammered. "Look—voyez. Candy—chocolate pour la petite mademwazelle."

The woman smiled and took the bar. "Merci, m'sieu—merci."

The major straightened up and turned away red-faced and muttering. He and the PFC drifted over to the counter to where the GI and the Driver still argued with the sergeant.

"That was high school French," said the major. "I really hadda dig deep for that one."

"She savvied it tho," said the PFC.

The major wanted to look back and see if the little girl was eating it. But he felt strangely embarrassed. The woman's eyes were very blue and clear. Her voice, when she spoke, sounded musical and very nice and odd in this madhouse of a terminal.

He screwed his face up into what he hoped was a major's proper and military expression and said to the sergeant: "Now look here, sergeant, I've sweated out a ride home for the last three days. When in hell am I EVER gonna get out . . ."

#20
CRASH

CRASH

CRASH

IT WAS at dusk at a base called Jorhat in lower Assam Valley. The air was balmy—not yet had the monsoon crept up with its stickiness, and the sun, while hot enough, still acted with moderate temper.

It was a beautiful dusk. The air was clear and everything stood out sharply as though etched. The RAF had put on a little show: two Hurricanes had hazed each other all over the sky, diving and then zooming, and finally they had landed hot and temperamental on their narrow undercarriages.

A visiting C-46 had waddled in and parked and settled down like a complacent, tired whale. The Assam shuttle—a dingy C-47—had just departed with its load of Yankee pilgrims bound for Chabua, and its passing left behind the same feeling of pleasant exhilaration as does the time-trusted departure of the 5:15 from the Junction.

There were eight or nine Drivers lounging on the porch of the roofed-over Operations bashie. Four of them had just returned from China. It had been a beautiful trip, they told several others. "CAVU," said one Driver. "For once I got a look at the rock pile. It's got anything I saw topped."

"You could see the Three Sisters clear as hell," said another.

"If only I'd had a cam'ra with color film," said a third. "Man, what pictures."

"Hear they have a good movie tonight," said a fourth.

"Yeh. Saw it last night. Wish I didn't have to go out. I could have had a date with an English nurse."

The Drivers lit cigarets and contentedly exhaled smoke and stared at the buzzards, which soared and circled over the native huts at the end of the runway.

"Must be something dead out there," remarked one.

"Naw. Just the way the Wogs always smell. The buzzards just watch 'em. If they move it means the time ain't right. If they stay still, the buzzards eat."

A C-87 slowly eased out to the end of the runway. The Drivers all watched it.

"Well anyway, it'll be a nice, moonlit night for those guys," said one.

"Someone was telling me that it's the last run for those two guys. They're due for home on rotation."

"Yeh—lucky bastards."

The group fell silent as the ship nosed down the runway and roared past them. It lifted and the gear began to sweep back into fuselage and wings. Suddenly a trail of smoke shot back. An icy hand squeezed down over their guts as the C-87, with awful steadiness, rolled to the left, inverted, and then plunged to the earth right on top of the native huts. There was a sudden booming sound and then a whoosh as 100-octane gasoline ignited . . .

#21
SACRED COWS IN THE EMPIRE'S SECOND CITY

SACRED COWS
IN THE EMPIRE'S
SECOND CITY!

SACRED COWS IN THE EMPIRE'S SECOND CITY

THERE WERE sacred cows in India, and Calcutta must have had the greatest number of them. They were of odd shapes and colors. They roamed the main boulevards and choked the winding, dung-carpeted alleyways.

They stalked the sidewalks and fought or made love on streetcar tracks and in the busiest intersections. Traffic and pedestrians had to give way to them. The natives and English burra sahibs paid them scarcely a glance. Only the few Drivers who on rare occasions managed to visit the big city stood and stared with wide-mouthed astonishment.

Occasionally, natives would furtively pat the animals, mutter prayers, and donate small offerings of food. Otherwise, many of the beasts could be seen hauling carts. And when the animals were so employed, the native drivers beat them unmercifully or else spurred them on by means of thrusting fingers into the plodding bovines' rectums.

Kipling once called Calcutta the "City of Dreadful Night." The Drivers found it just as dreadful by day. At least the hours of darkness hid the livid, leprous complexion of the city. The brassy sun sardonically revealed everything, and its heat brought forth the stench.

Daylight would reveal the thin, racked multitudes; the festering piles of rancid garbage; the cloth-covered, reclining figures who slept on the pavement oblivious of traffic and passersby.

The sun would display the endless, thin-flanked ricksha wallahs weaving in and around motorized traffic; the ancient, wheezing, asthmatic taxis with their bearded, piratical Sikh drivers; the holy men and women.

The holy people were another source of bemusement to the Drivers. There was one of them—a wild-eyed, bearded, bushy-haired creature of undetermined age who, unmolested, stalked the main thoroughfares. He was stark naked, and he wore a chain and spike fastened to his genitalia. The Drivers used to get pictures of him with their cameras. Sometimes he posed with a smile; occasionally he broke into wild, thin shrieks of rage.

There was a girl—fairly attractive too. She had a sleek, brown skin and beautiful breasts. Her features were even and extremely delicate. She used to lie in the centers of busy streets and comb her hair and sing like the fabled Lorelie. The Drivers, with a rare directness, called her "Bare-Assed Betty."

She liked to smile and wave at passing trucks, jeeps, and rickshas. But if anyone stopped to take pictures, she would spit like a cat, throw rocks, and dart off. One night Betty chose to sleep on the Grand Trunk highway, which led from Calcutta to Hastings Mill, where the Air Forces had its headquarters. A convoy of six-by-six trucks, driving under dim-out restrictions, came boring down the road. The next morning they found Betty—

But Calcutta had other things for the starry-eyed Drivers who came down from the wilds of Assam to dip into civilization's fleshpots. There was the Grand Hotel—a ramshackle, rat-infested structure with high-ceilinged rooms, fans, and honest-to-God bathtubs.

For the higher rankers there were more-modern, cleaner rooms in Calcutta's finest hotel—the Great Eastern. Here could even be found a dazzling, glass-bespangled, air-conditioned dining room. And in this wonderful establishment, one could procure ice cream (if one did not mind toying with the eventuality of amoebic or cholera).

The Drivers used to brazenly heckle the billeting sergeants of the Great Eastern and manage, on occasion, to procure a room. Sometimes five or six of them shared one room.

Those were wonderful moments. The Moslem room bearers would stand by and watch with religious horror while the Drivers, stripped to the skin, ordered big, "burra" brandies and soda and lay on the beds and watched the ceiling fans.

The boys would talk to the bearers.

"Amrikans are big and strong," they'd tell the thin Indians. "Know why?"

The Indians would smile and shrug. "Why, sahib?"

"Because we stand up when we pee. Not like you guys. You squat."

The Indians would think about it. It was true. Indian males always squatted when they relieved themselves. It was a national pastime. Even along the brightest and busiest of Calcutta's boulevards could be seen rows of men squatting with their backs to traffic. Of course only the lower castes did this, never the Brahmins or Parsees.

Many Indians believed the Drivers and began to stand up. They would call the attention of their women to this phenomenon and would explain that they were going to become big and strong, like the "Amrikans."

For amusement, the Drivers could go to the British-and-American Officers' Club. That was a nightclub managed by an olive-skinned, sauve ex-American who, so gossip had it, was wanted by the FBI for income tax evasion or murder or kidnapping or something equally as fascinating.

The B&A Club was the most popular rendezvous. Here men met who had counted one another dead or missing according to rumor and hearsay: here they came with their dates—bright-eyed, writhing-hipped, passionate Anglo-Indian girls. Here one could sometimes get scotch whiskey or dance to a small orchestra and eat water-buffalo steaks that had hung long enough and had become rotten enough to be almost palatable.

There was also Firpo's Restaurant—a huge, two-story affair. Many preferred Firpo's. Enlisted men could come there, and the Drivers frequently liked to be with their crew chiefs and radio operators. Besides, rumor also had it that the proprietor, Firpo, was likewise an American, although he did not seem to have any gangster background.

The American Calcutta headquarters was the Hindustan Building—a multistoried, semimodern structure. Here the Army Ground Force had established a large Post Exchange replete with ice-cold coca-colas, Stateside hamburgers, tobacco, cigarets, and candy. It smelled, sounded, and looked like home. There was even a jukebox in the corner, and if one were lucky, one might meet a nurse or a Red Cross girl and get a date—

The American and the Royal Air Forces shared a rambling jute mile, about 18 miles up the Hooghly River from Calcutta proper.

When the owners had leased it to the armed forces to become a combination headquarters and living establishment, most of the machinery had been taken out. All that was left were huge wheels and pulleys that clung to the dingy ceilings.

Lieutenant General Stratemeyer had been the genius behind the move from New Delhi to Hastings Mill. The general desired that the Army Air Forces and the RAF live together like one happy family.

Officers and enlisted men found themselves quartered in past factory compartments. There were no fans at first. The lights did not work properly, and the monsoon heat was multiplied ninefold. A few went raving mad. And the rest, watching the madmen, wished they could also blow their tops and thus obtain some measure of relief.

But, gradually, the fans came and were installed; the food got a little better and everyone became used to the sewage smell that hung over the place like an invisible, suffocating cloud. In time, "Strat," as he was endearingly called by his immediate associates, beamed with approval from the porch of his two-story separate home, which was located on a lawn near the river. The PX was full: the officers' club was nicely decorated with chrome-and-leather furniture. Even the GIs had their own club and bar, and, besides, there were a bunch of Wacs coming in—everything was lovely—

As a rule, every Driver was sympathetic to the Indian's cause—at first. It seems that all Americans were willing to passionately and immediately side with all and sundry "underdogs." And, certainly, there had been lots of pro-Indian propaganda spread and repeated, no doubt by a few sincere people as well as pro-Japanese Indians.

The British were the heels. The Limeys were no goddamn good. The lousy English were exploiting the poor, downtrodden, brow-beaten Wogs.

That was how the average Driver felt until he had a good opportunity to study India. Then he found out something else.

The British—some of them—WERE exploiters. But they were not half as vicious, overbearing, and untrustworthy as the high-caste Indian himself.

The Driver saw the callousness of Indian toward Indian; he stared at the sacred cows and the holy people; he stood by and watched the stupefying, barbaric spectacle of the Juggernaut Festival and realized, with a start, that India's troubles were strictly her own. The British, in a mere two hundred years, could not have stultified human beings as efficiently as the Indians had done to one another over a period of centuries. He began to suspect that the Brahmin desperately needed the shield of Hindu worship as a bulwark for a caste system that permitted a social system of inequality that was darker than the Middle Ages.

It was amazing—how a fortnight of leave in the City of Dreadful Night could show him all this so much better than printed words and talk . . .

#22
LOADING IN ASSAM

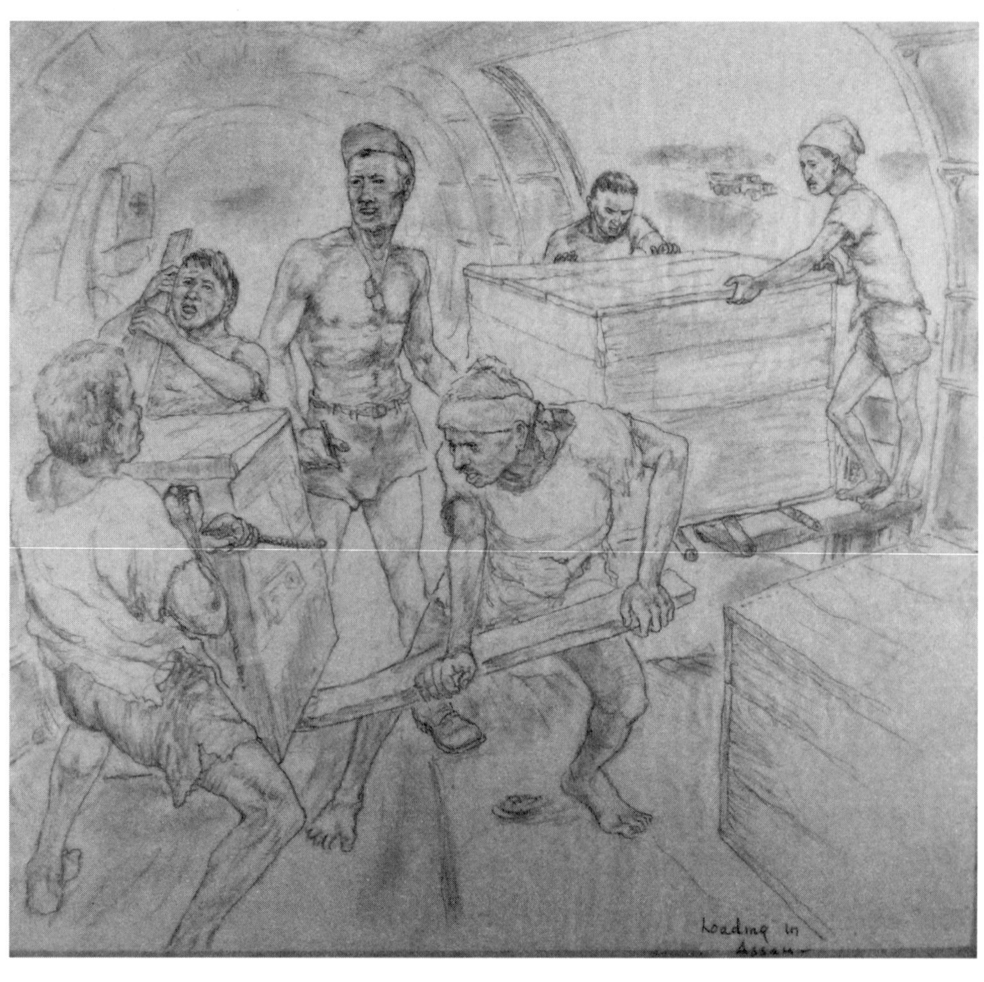
Loading in
Assam

LOADING IN ASSAM

THE FAT-BELLIED C-46s (Commandoes, they were called) were always hungry for cargo, and the half-naked Wog coolies who had been recruited by the British to load the planes looked as though they had barely enough energy for life itself, let alone the shifting and lifting of boxes, crates, bombs, and engines.

But tug, shove, pry, and lift they did. Six-by-six trucks, loaded with the myriad things that went across the Hump, roared to revetments, and the coolies, pushed, bullied, and cajoled by half-nude GIs, stuffed the airplanes.

The heat outside hit 120 degrees and more. But inside, the airplane outhelled hell. GIs helped tug and strain, and the sweat rolled off glistening flanks and muscle-ridged shoulders.

The coolies chanted their sing-song lament: "Ey-sah: ey-SAH!" And a 1,000-pound, crated Allison engine slowly moved up the inclined floor to its mooring place.

The floors were rough and splintered. And time and again, coolies with crushed toes and bleeding feet, with black eyes brightened by pain, reported to their GI supervisor: "Sahhb—sahhb. Look!"

The GI would swear and wave his arms, but he quickly rushed the coolie to aid. And many of the GIs got to know their coolies and liked them and felt very sorry for them. At least the GI knew that the war would someday end and the Hump would be a thing of the past, but the poor coolie, the dismal, dumb, stupid bastard—the poor Wog, God help him—he had to STAY in India . . .

#23
HIGHWAY TRAFFIC NEAR KUNMING

HIGHWAY TRAFFIC NEAR KUNMING

CHINA SEEMED, to the Drivers, to be a vast graveyard. From the air, one peered through the cockpit windshield down upon acres and acres of tiny little hummocks that looked like haystacks. These were graves, and they simply pockmarked the reddish earth that composed the Yunnan Plateau.

The roads that wandered through the hills and along the lakes were rock-filled and took a costly toll of auto and truck engines, gears, and tires. And every road was lined with these graves. Some of the hummocks had large stone markers with weather-beaten, partly obliterated Chinese characters carved thereon. But the majority of the graves were unmarked. The occupants were unknown and, mostly, one with the rich, red earth.

During the heavy rains, many of the graves came apart, and then the passing traffic would have a fine assortment of skulls and pelvis, thigh, and shin bones to contemplate.

The old timers explained that in the earlier days it was hard to undertake any new construction. The Chinese were superstitious about desecrating the graves of their ancestors. But the Hump Drivers wondered about that because the Chinese they encountered did not seem to have any compunction whatever about kicking a skull out of the way whenever the occasion warranted it.

The living Chinese filled the highways that led in and out of Kunming, or Chanyi or Luliang. Many of them rode in ancient, rattling, charcoal-burning trucks and buses. Others used little donkeys.

The American trucks fascinated and frightened the Chinese. The huge, olive-drab six-by-six trucks with the white stars painted on the engine hoods seemed to petrify them.

Whenever a single vehicle or a convoy came roaring and lurching over the rutted roads, the Chinese would crowd to the side and blink with half-pleading, half-frightened little smiles for consideration.

The GIs who drove the trucks liked to speed, but rarely did they hit any of the Chinese or their animals.

It was the fear that amused the American truck drivers. They had such complete self-confidence in their ability to handle these giant vehicles that the Chinese doubts and fright evoked their laughter and produced a desire to show off. “Lookit them chicken bastards,” the kids would scoff. “Can yuh ’magine ’em walkin’ acrosst Broadway—or down Wilshire Boulevard in Los Angeles!”

And then they would display their remarkable skill and whisk by as closely as they could to the cowering Chinese and roar with amusement when human and animal alike bolted off into the rice paddies—

#24
"TRANSPORTATION IS HERE, LOOTENINT"

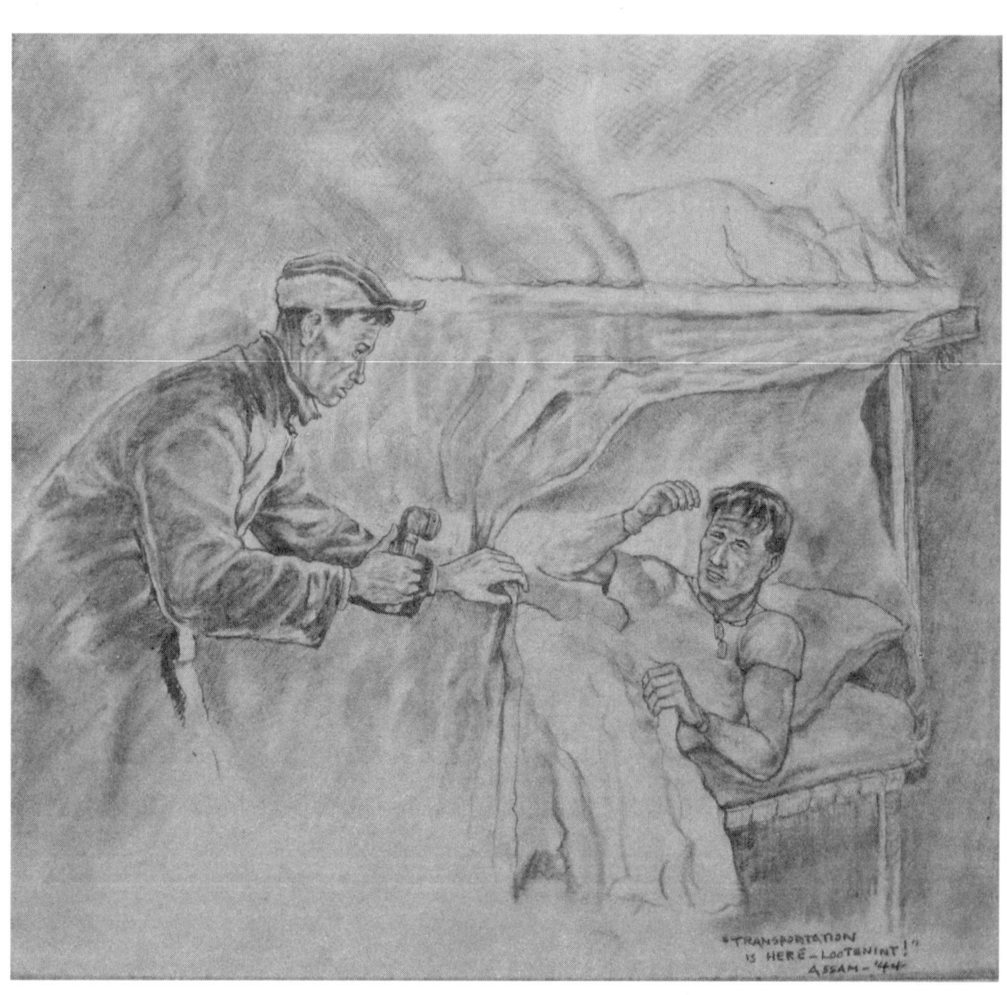
"TRANSPORTATION
IS HERE – LOOTENINT!"
ASSAM – '44

"TRANSPORTATION IS HERE, LOOTENINT"

THE COLD, unfriendly eye of a flashlight brings you out of a restless, tortured sleep. The CQ's (Charge of Quarters') hand is immediately withdrawn from beneath the mosquito netting, and his voice, far away to your sleep-befuddled ears, murmurs: "Transportation is here."

The bed feels damp, almost slimy, and the stench of rotting bamboo makes you very depressed. Outside you can hear rain dripping from the eaves while, from far off, comes the guttural protest of engines being warmed up. You switch on your own flashlight and note the time: "Jezus—two o'clock."

The soggy pancakes and coffee you consumed short hours before weigh heavily on your stomach as you slowly, reluctantly swing your legs over the side of the creaking charpoy and grope for heavy GI shoes and socks.

Although the heat is oppressive, you shudder because of the dampness of your clothing. You gather your gear, a .45 automatic, web pistol belt, jungle knife—a canteen of tepid, chlorinated water. You check your flight jacket and make sure that the pockets contain water-proofed matches, a small sack of salt (for leeches, in case you should have to bail over the jungle), two spare packs of cigarets, and a couple of bars of D-ration chocolate. Then you tiptoe so as not to awaken the other sleepers, and step outside the bashie and into the waiting Command car.

The ride to the field is made in silence. You've acknowledged the presence of the rest of the crew by means of mere grunts. The rain changes from a drizzle to a downpour. Now your clothing is really wet.

As the car nears the field, the lights of the freight sheds flicker through the monsoon. Groups of coolies sweat at heavy cargo and chant monotonously: "Ey-SAH, Ey-SAH," as they inch huge crates across the slimy platforms toward waiting six-by-six trucks. And then you have passed the sheds, and the operations building, with its revolving beacon futily trying to pierce the rain, appears before you.

The operations officers' garrulous geniality does not set well.

"Ready to get the show on the road, huh." His laugh makes you study his features, with an eye toward rearranging them.

You check the weather and try to wipe the clown from your mind. The weather is the same: icing up to 14,000 feet—perhaps higher: heavy stuff over the First Ridge. You reach for the clearance sheet and begin to fill it out. An arriving crew describes difficulties encountered with their radio compasses. Snatches of their conversation drift toward you as you stride to the coffee shack.

"There I was when BOTH of the guddamned compasses went tuh-DOINK! Christ—"

The coffee, while tasteless, warms you up inside. You light a cigaret and stare idly at your companions. "'Nother day . . . 'nother dollar," says one of them. He looks incongruous in his half-costume, half-uniform getup. His jockey flight cap is thrust back, and the peak slopes upward in a 45-degree, jaunty angle. He is clad in disheveled cottons. His shirt is minus any insignia. In the air he will—along with you and everyone else—start putting on layers of clothing, coveralls and then flight jackets, as the temperature drops with increasing altitude.

The radio operator toys with his oxygen mask. Its hose whips flaccidly, like the trunk of a small elephant. He makes a certain gesture with it. The thing DOES resemble a phallus. It is no longer funny to you, but he is a good kid and he loves to get a response, so you laugh and make the apropos obscene remark.

Now you sweat out maintenance. At the last minute they told you that the left engine was being checked for a magneto drop.

"Hell, it'll take hours," says one of the crew. "We coulda stayed in our sacks."

"TRANSPORTATION IS HERE, LOOTENINT"

The same old bitches, the same endless waiting. You sit and smoke cigarets and stare at the black, black wet night and try to keep from thinking.

And then the crew chief arrives and says that the plane is as ready as she'll ever be. "Yuh might notice kind of a big drop in the lef' engine when y'run 'er up," he says almost apologetically, "but that's jus' moisture. This dam monsoon. She'll clear up topside."

You ride in an Operations jeep to the revetment, where the ship hulks darkly, its bulging sides gleaming in the headlights of the saucy, tiny vehicle. There is a lone GI in the cabin finishing the tie-down of the cargo. A truck with natives, their loading chore finished, stands by.

The rain has stopped and there is that familiar smell of warm oil and stale rainwater slowly cooking on hot asphalt. You walk around the ship, peer into the wheel wells, scan the tires. There is a last-minute urge for relief, and you are one of several shadowy figures on the lee side of the empennage.

"When I get home," says one shadow, "I'd better watch myself. Helluva note to get off a Stateside passenger ship and leak in front of God an' everybody."

A chuckle greets this. It really is funny. You think of your speech and mannerisms. You've really lived as you've always wanted to as a boy—away from apron-string influences. Bathe when you feel like it, piss off the front porch of the bashie—drink hot, stale beer and cuss and shout and pass gas and, in general, not give a good guddam.

It's the life little boys always dream of: a fairy land where hookey is esteemed, bathtubs are smashed, and time doesn't count, and there are no mothers and big sisters to scold and monitor. You grunt with self-derision and swing up into the ship.

The GI has left and the cargo is in place, and you notice the yellow USAAF manifests as you squeeze by and enter the cockpit up front. The radio operator slips into his cubbyhole, and the copilot fiddles with his long legs and adjusts his rudder pedals and seat.

Now it is all business. A faint voice, the crew chief's, shouts: "Clear on the right!"

You unhurriedly go through the checklist; flip the master switch, the inverter; turn on your Command radio receiver. The copilot advances the fuel mixture control to "Lean," and your hand rests on the energizer switches. "Clear on the right," you finally echo. The engine begins to hum in a tone that becomes louder and higher. Your hand jams the energizer switch to "start." Reluctantly the prop turns, gears clash, and then with a cough and gasp the engine takes hold. Now you nurse the throttle—the engine clears its throat and settles to a steady growl. The instrument panel shakes and jiggles. The airplane is beginning to take on its own strange type of life. You repeat the procedure with the left engine. The crew chief, below, holds up one hand with the thumb and forefinger prescribing a circle, and then he ducks out of sight.

The copilot has been busy with the radio. His voice, flattened in that curious, stylized monotone, has requested and received the tower's permission for you to move into position for engine warm-up and takeoff.

His left hand flicks down, removes the tailwheel lock. You jiggle your feet, and, straining your eyes ahead, you gingerly advance the throttles. The engines snarl and the plane protestingly inches forward. Your right toe depresses a brake, and the left engine is revved up. The ship slowly waddles to the right while the brakes squeak and groan, and the plane, like a huge, disgruntled water buffalo, waddles down the slippery taxi strip to the warm-up apron.

There you lock the brakes and settle down to the business at hand. The throttles are thrust forward, singly, and the tremendous power of your engines bellows against the night while your hands flick switches and your eyes scan the disinterested faces of the instrument dials. Contrary to what the crew chief had said, there is no indication of mag trouble, and for that you are briefly elated.

Now the copilot queries the tower for permission to take off. You swing the ship to the left, and she finally sits contemplating the long, black runway with its boundaries marked by fitful, weak lights. The radio operator and crew chief stand right behind. You can feel their breath coming on the back of your neck. Your landing lights flick on, and they etch a few figures: bunched coolies with dark and spindly loins; an Indian soldier, his steel helmet and bayonet brightly reflecting the glaring eyes of the ship. You check to make sure the tailwheel is locked. Through force of habit, you again move the controls, wheel, and rudder to full travel to make doubly sure that the rudder, elevator, and aileron blocks have been removed—and then your hand gently eases the throttles forward.

The engines take hold and the plane, no longer a buffalo, becomes something else. The runway lights begin to flick past on either side. The air takes hold of the rudder. The nose swings slightly to the left, and a gentle pressure against the right rudder pedal brings it back and holds it dead center. The tension mounts, and with it comes an odd ecstasy of speed and power. Your right wrist is tapped gently—the copilot has taken over the throttles.

Now you grasp the wheel and ease back on the elevator trim tab. Abruptly the oncoming black runway strip falls beneath you. You jerk your thumb, and eager hands cause the gear to rise. For a moment the nose settles and then it points upward. You see the red boundary lights flit beneath, and then you flip off the landing lights. Now, ahead are only your dimly glowing instruments.

Thus there begins the work of the trip. The throttles are set for proper climbing power—the props are adjusted to deliver the most advantageous amount of revolutions per minute that will enable your heavily laden ship to climb and climb and climb. Meanwhile, you watch that miniature airplane on your instrument panel and control your ship so that it ascends in a gradual spiral that keeps you over Assam and yet enables you to get many thousands of feet of clean air between yourself and the jagged peaks of the First Ridge.

Finally you straighten out. Now it is eastward that you run, straight, clean, and unfettered. The engines settle down to an even roar that quickly is pushed by familiarity into the subconscious. You are concerned only with the progress of the flight—reaching a broadcast radio checkpoint. It is important to reach that station at the time you have forecast. That is the only way in which you can determine whether the winds are behind or ahead of you.

You note the air speed and outside air temperature and fiddle with the complicated calculator, which is really a circular slide rule. Your hands and eyes—and those of the copilot—constantly check the radio receivers, prowling for news from this range station or that homing beacon—tiny, man-devised motes of communication that help lance the awful, black void that is the Hump.

The steady climb has made you relax a little. And with a start, you notice from the face of the altimeter that the time has come to put into action the supercharging mechanism that enables your engines to breathe more freely and perform better at high altitude. You do this chore and notice that the air is drier and cold. The crew chief lights a last cigaret before going on oxygen. The smoke makes you hungry and you light up as well, and your cigaret glow casts many orange reflections on the windshield.

The plane lurches—rides smoothly and then shudders. It is the overcast. To make sure, you momentarily turn on the landing lights. The beams show whirling, murky stuff that rushes with frightful speed right into your face and twists and winds back from the blunt snout of the ship. It is as though you were standing still in the midst of a river of flowing, engulfing ectoplasm.

For an instant you get a weird feeling of suspension in a foreign universe, and then the radio compass needle swings and points to the right. You note the time and nod to the copilot.

"Right on the button," you yell. "That was Shing."

Now you put on your flight jacket because it's getting really cold. The crew chief fiddles around with the cockpit heat. You remember what they say about oxygen starvation, and you douse the cigaret and put the big mask on your face and begin to blubber. It has a rubbery, sweaty smell, and your chin begins to itch.

The overcast is moderately rough. Once in a while the ship twitches as though ridding itself of annoying insects; the next instant she rides heavily from one wave of air to the next. The crew chief has gone back, and his flashlight plays fitfully around the engine nacelles. He is questing for ice, but that arch enemy does not make an appearance.

You become aware of an odd glow ahead—your eyes rise from the instruments to the windshield, and in that instant the ship's nose has contemptuously thrust aside the last wisps of cloud, and now you find yourself soaring above a vast, unending sea of cumulus while, overhead, a full moon rides in aloof introspection . . .

#25
COLORED STILWELL DRIVERS

COLORED Stillwell-Road drivers
SWEATING OUT A SHIP IN KUNMING—

COLORED STILWELL DRIVERS

WHEN THEY began to bring colored troops into Assam, a lot of high rank got nervous. They could see only racial strife, and so these military "segregationists" spread a lot of confused "word-of-mouth" directives throughout the area.

For a long time, the "Wheels" claimed the Nationalist government of China refused to permit American Negro troops into the Kunming area. And when the Mars Men finally smashed through Burma (finishing up what the tired Marauders had started and halfway accomplished), the Stilwell Road was completed and a Terrible Problem Arose Overnight.

The men who were to drive the truck convoys to China were colored soldiers for the most part. The Chinese were in a dilemma. The American brass hats were in a quandary. Finally, an extraordinary operation was devised. The convoy would come to China. There would be much fanfare. White officers and enlisted men would be wined and dined, but the "niggers" would be herded into C-46s and shot, posthaste, back to Assam. There they would be thrown into another convoy and so on, ad nauseam.

The Drivers knew what was happening, and they were sore because those colored boys really put out. They had helped build the road from Ledo despite malaria, blood-sucking leeches, wild elephants, and occasional Jap snipers. And driving the road was a chore—a rugged one. Lots of trucks rolled down 1,000-foot inclines—and many colored boys went with them—and the Hump Drivers knew that a black skin covered a stout heart that pumped red blood—as red as the blood of any white man.

At first the Negroes were pushed around, but hatred and stupidity cannot prevail for long. For every high-ranking stinker there are at least a few decent, high-ranking white men who feel and act in a manner befitting their traditions, background, and authority.

So they finally succeeded in letting the colored drivers wander through Kunming and stare fascinatedly at the ordinary Chinese, who stared back with equal fascination. It was a good thing that they let these boys stretch their legs a bit. It was pretty difficult to explain to the ordinary Chinaman how America was against Fascism only to have this selfsame Chinaman—the knob-headed, goddamn dumbbell—come back with "But I do not understand! For instance—look how you treat your Negro soldiers! Are they not Americans? Are they not part of your army?"

Ah—those dam' Slopies!

But the Drivers who flew the colored boys back to India liked them. It was wonderful to watch these lads—short and tall, fat and skinny—lounge with that amazing indolence of their race.

It was a comfort to hear their accents in fervent argument or else in the technicalities of wine, women, dice, and poker. It was a friendly, homely, heartening potpourri of Harlem, the Deep South, and the West.

Alas, though, a simple Hump Driver was just an ordinary guy. He could get along nicely with the Stilwell Road Driver. It was so difficult for him to understand the Wheels—or act like a Wheel—

#26
THE EGGUS SHACK

GET CHOW
TICKETS AT
OPERATIONS
REMEMBER
40 MINUTES!
UNLOAD
AND GET
GOING!!

THE EGGUS SHACK

THE DRIVERS could always look forward to one thing: "eggus" in China.

Down in Assam, fresh eggs were practically nonexistent, while powdered eggs were few and frowned upon. At first mess, officers and sergeants used to buy eggs on the open market, but the British tea plantation owners were alarmed because the Americans paid more, and, consequently, the Wogs raised the prices. So the tea planters complained to the "Wheels" and said that there would be a shortage of provisions if the Drivers continued to buy Assam eggs. Consequently the Wheels ordered the mess boys to lay off, and, as a result the Drivers got nothing except C ration, Spam, and other things too horrible to relate.

But there were eggus in China, and the gang always looked forward to a few minutes of rest while the airplanes were being unloaded. The rest and hot, black, and bitter coffee and the eggs—two, four, and sometimes six eggs either "sklambelled" or "flied."

The eggus shacks were run by Chinese, of course, and one just did not venture into the kitchen. It would do no good to see a cook with open, pus-ridden sores handling food with his hands. Nor would the sight of dropped bread retrieved from the rat-prowled floors help any.

The eggus shack was generally a madhouse. It was always jammed, and men bolted their food and gulped the coffee, because the credo was hurry and get unloaded. Eat and beat it back to Assam. Every minute on the ground was wasted.

So the Drivers hurried and rushed back to their ships and took off into the treacherous black night and worried over instruments and weather. Their eggs and coffee and bread that tasted like straw lay in an unhappy, fermenting mass in their bellies and gave them heartburn, indigestion, and a general feeling of unhappiness.

There was a young colonel who became commanding officer of the China Wing. He stood in the eggus shack one night and watched the Drivers, and his fine, patrician nose wrinkled.

"Pigs," he snorted. "Look at them. They eat and act like pigs."

His aide watched the Drivers gobble their food, jostle one another (the room could hold ten comfortably, and there were at least fifty jammed into it), and weave in and out of the place. The air was hot and humid and jammed with the odor of frying grease and tobacco smoke.

"Sir," ventured the aide. "I'm afraid that there is neither time nor room for proper—er—table manners."

"Nonsense. They are just irresponsible. They act like pigs here because that is their natural inclination. They've had no proper background at all. If I had my way about it, I'd relieve most of them of their commissions!"

The colonel and his aide went outside and entered the 1942 deluxe Plymouth four-door sedan that had been assigned to him as a staff car.

The colonel and a select few of his staff dwelt in a huge, rambling, brand-new mansion in the very nicest (which meant the place that smelled the least offensive) part of Kunming.

The driver, a sergeant, maintained a steady, sedate pace, and the colonel and his aide swept into the entrance of the house, which had been erected for the state-occasion use of the commanding general of the India-China Division of the Air Transport Command whenever he swept into Kunming on his private, staff airplane—a C-54 four-engined job.

The colonel enjoyed the service of a very fine mess sergeant and cook. The cook had worked for a swanky Los Angeles hotel as a chef in peacetime, and he could accomplish wonders. He could make Spam and C ration delectable, but he rarely had to do that because there was generally a nice steak of steak and chops and other delicacies available.

The colonel and his staff, of course, had their predinner, iced highball or else cold beer, and then, in the beautiful dining room, he told his assistants (all lieutenant colonels) about what awful pigs most of the Drivers were . . .

#27
AMERICANS BUYING PEANUTS

LAVOVE
AMERICANS BUYING
PEANUTS IN A
CHINESE VILLAGE

AMERICANS BUYING PEANUTS

KIDS ARE kids no matter where they live, the color of their skin, or their religion.

Chinese kids are no different than American kids. They play the same games: hide-and-go-seek, marbles, and tag. And they were very curious about Americans—"Megwas" and especially fliers, who, to those bright, stant-eyed kids, were Megwa fiji bings—American flying soldiers.

The grown-up Chinese were curious too. And invariably a crowd of kids with an adult or two would gather while one or two Drivers stood and gawked into curio shops or else bought pounds and pounds of roasted peanuts from quilt-coated vendors.

No matter what the Drivers did, it would bring forth laughs, excited comment, and very intent scrutiny.

Whenever a Driver offered a kid some peanuts, everyone would laugh and little taloned hands would grab.

The Chinese grown-ups like their children, and when the Drivers were nice to the kids, the grown-ups chuckled and talked rapidly to each other and nodded with approval. Even ancient, withered men, sucking on their long pipes, would grin, fleetingly, and make satisfied sounds.

The peanuts were good and safe to eat. They were much tastier, for instance, than C ration or Spam or any of the other edible monstrosities that Stateside science had produced with a fine smugness.

So to the kids and grown-ups, the sight of Megwa fiji bings buying pounds of peanuts and stuffing them into pockets of flight jackets and coveralls was very funny and reassuring. Because no one could really fear these young-old men with their tired faces, who stuffed themselves with goobers and chatted and laughed at the kids and threw handfuls to them. Even the heavy, dull-blue .45 automatic pistols hanging from their belts did not throw any fear into the kids.

The Chinese kids laughed easily and always acted like kids in spite of their thinness and cold and hunger. The Indian kids generally whined for baksheesh or stood around with sullen faces.

The Drivers rarely encountered a Slopie kid who begged for anything more valuable than, occasionally, a "cigalet."

But those dam' Wog kids were always begging . . .

#28
AN ASSAM EVENING

AN ASSAM EVENING
'44

AN ASSAM EVENING

IT WAS generally hot and very, very sticky. Sweat just collected and ran, and the mold got into everything, and leather and clothing and bedding stank.

Sometimes it was too hot to eat. Frequently it was too hot for any sleep, and Drivers sat up and played cards or read and reread old books, newspapers, and magazines until their heads drooped from utter exhaustion. And then they would bat their way through clouds of the damndest-looking Assam bugs and crawl into the smothering, steaming embrace of their charpoys and mosquito nets.

Little things often provoked snarling comment and arguments. Sometimes there would be a hasty punch or two exchanged. But those instances were rather rare, and, besides, they were quickly hushed up. The brass, down in their fan-equipped headquarters at Calcutta or New Delhi, did not understand how nerves could be frazzled. The "Wheels" had good food and comfort. Why, they not only had cold beer and ice for their mixed drinks, they even could have cold cokes and ice cream.

But the Drivers could not get those things: 99 percent of them had only their occasional issue of hot beer—and memories.

That and, of course, flying the Hump. But they were officers, and if the "Wheels" in New Delhi and Calcutta heard how two of these wilted, exhausted, nervous wrecks had, in a sudden explosion of frustration, punched one another in the nose, why that was conduct unbecoming an officer and gentleman. And it meant a court-martial with a heavy fine. In several cases the military tribunals actually gave men dishonorable discharges and jail sentences.

There was a captain whose first name was Matt. He was a southerner—hot blooded, gallant, and a very brave man because 'way down deep he was afraid of the Hump and, consequently, drove himself twice as hard as any other Driver. Once he had crossed the Hump twice in twenty-four hours. And this was done in the early, deadly days, when the route lay far to the north of Fort Hertz, where the mountains are highest and the winds the most treacherous.

But one night Matt's temper exploded—it was a little thing, really, and the Driver he walloped was not actually hurt—perhaps a black eye. But his commanding officer put him into solitary confinement in his own quarters. He could leave his insect-ridden bashie only to eat his meals or go to the latrine.

Everyone was ordered to keep away from Matt's quarters, and so everyone sneaked by at night and poked in notes and secretly shared whatever they had in the way of books and liquor and food and sympathy. That went on for three months, and then they moved him down to Calcutta, where a court-martial told him that he was a disgrace, that he would be fined a lot of money, and that he would either be given a discharge without honor or else reduced in rank from captain to second lieutenant. He had the Air Medal and the Distinguished Flying Cross. His nerves were shot. He had done a terrific job. But he now felt like a criminal.

Fortunately for him, his folks at home were influential. So he was merely fined, according to subsequent rumor. But there were lots of other hot evenings in Assam, and Drivers, both commissioned and enlisted, were tossed by the "Wheels" into the Great, Smug, Dumb, Lofty Hopper and crushed and broken. Only these young-oldsters came from ordinary folks in the States, who had no significance or influence, so they were out of luck.

One sometimes wonders what goes on in a man's mind after he has shot his wad and then found himself, because of a silly little thing, stripped of his self-respect and painted in a criminal, dishonorable light . . .

#29
TAXIING

FOLLOW
ME
TAXIING –

TAXIING

NEITHER KUNMING nor any of the Assam fields were places that anyone in his right mind would want to consider "home." But to weary Drivers, the home base was a wonderful place to reach at the end of a run.

Flying an airplane takes quite a lot out of a person—especially if weather conditions have been rough, instruments erratic, and radio navigational aids unreliable or (as was often the case) nonexistent.

And while the pilots, radio operators, and crew chiefs did not actually notice any change in their feelings, there was a certain amount of tenseness that had accumulated during the flight. This tenseness was actually an accumulation of nervous energy that had built up and the minute the landing 'plane had stopped its roll and the copilot unlocked the tall wheel so that it could turn off the runway and nose toward a revetment, all that nervous energy demanded an outlet.

It manifested itself on different Drivers in different ways. Some were garrulous and felt an inclination to laugh at things that were not at all humorous. Others became irritable and were liable to snap someone's head off at the least provocation.

No one—except at odd moments and always with mild surprise—paid any attention to the beads of sweat that collected around lips and beneath eyes. Nor did anyone ever really notice how the palms of one's hands ran wet with perspiration.

But it was always a relief, no matter how devoted one was to flying, to slowly taxi toward the waiting revetment with its little duster of trucks and maintenance and unloading personnel. Ahead chugged the little jeep with the beckoning "follow-me" sign perched on its rear end. The pilot would slowly inch his ship ahead, watching carefully from his side lest his wingtip brush another. The radio operator and crew chief meanwhile gathered up their belongings, and the copilot would fuss with little, last-minute details that did not really amount to anything. It was mostly a way of easing off that built-up pressure.

And when the ship finally came to a stop and the props clattered into silence, everyone sat for a moment in a strange, momentary vacuum that had no time, no significance: merely a far-off, blue-study stare, while a dim feeling of regret and relief flickered at the same time.

The signing of the Form One was both a ritual and a blessing. It was a solemn attestation to the fact that the Drivers had flown so many hours and fractions thereof; that they had made a certain number of takeoffs and landings. Judiciously the crew would consult over the engineering part of the report form. Seriously and slowly, the crew chief would explain deficiencies of mechanism. The first pilot would nod; the copilot would add his complaints and, finally, the whole thing would be entered for the maintenance gang to study and perhaps repair or correct.

And when this solemn pact had been signed, everyone dashed out of the airplane and suddenly felt almost like kids let out of school . . .

#30
SLOPIE TROOPS ON THE MOVE

SLOPY TROOPS ON
The Move—

SLOPIE TROOPS ON THE MOVE

FOR YEARS, before the young-old men had become Drivers, they had heard and read about the brave Chinese.

Their admiration had been prefabricated by writers like Pearl Buck and, during the early twenties, Floyd Gibbons. They had formed mental images of stalwart, ivory-skinned men and women—rugged with just the proper rakish amount of sophisticated raggedness that Hollywood extras assume: cheerful and smiling—stoic in the face of danger and warmly human in between heroic stands.

The generalissimo and the madame were, to the Drivers-to-be, deities. Did they not stand for the ultimate in self-sacrifice and devotion and loyalty to the tenets of Freedom and Democracy!

But all that was before the Drivers came over the Hump and saw and smelled and put two and two together.

Oh, the generals and colonels and all the cheerful, solemn, happy, comfortable, well-padded staff people spoke ringingly of the wonderful Resistance. But still the Japs advanced whenever they chose, and Kweilin fell, as did Liuchow and Nanning and many more places.

But the Drivers, when they saw the long lines of plodding troops that filed alongside the roads near Kunming, realized how absurd all that stuff was. How could human beings, thin and tottering, freezing in cotton, equipped with ancient weapons—with the pinch of hunger on face and loin—how could such as these resist anything!

Of course the Drivers realized other things. For instance, there were the concentration camps—especially the one on the outskirts of Hsian.

There was the story of a couple of Drivers who had to bail out and who were "rescued" by a Nationalist column. These Drivers were stripped of everything they owned and treated like prisoners. When the Nationalist column was wiped out by a Communist detachment, the Americans were returned to the Kunming area. And because one of the Drivers had kept a diary recording the treatment he and his companions had received at the hands of the Nationalists, they had to be rushed to America and safety—lest the Nationalist secret police get to them. The Drivers learned all about these and many other things that turned most of their minds and hearts bitterly against the "Noble Allies" and their leaders. But still they flew the Hump and fulfilled their missions. They did what was asked of them, even if they knew it was futile and that theirs was a forgotten contribution to a forgotten Front.

And what the Drivers did was a hell of a lot more than what the Noble Allies did . . .

#31
CALCUTTA TAXI WALLAHS

CALCUTTA
TAXI
WALLAHS

CALCUTTA TAXI WALLAHS

IN THE first place, Drivers generally started with the premise that most Wogs were thieves, swindlers, liars, and cheats.

Furthermore, since there were different types of Wogs, there were differing degrees of orneriness. The Bengali, for example, were worse than the Mahrattas, and the Sikhs were the worst of the lot.

Especially in Calcutta, where the Sikhs monopolized the taxi cab business.

The cabs themselves were remarkable displays of sheer mechanical genius. It took a magician's touch, after all, to keep the wheezing, asthmatic 1924 and '25 model Oakland and Studebaker touring-car taxicabs chugging day in and day out.

Fresh-Air cabs, the Drivers called them. And since the huge, swarthy, bearded, turbaned Sikh driver rarely drove without a counterpart seated on his left—it was assumed by the pleasure-bent, Hump-happy Drivers that the cabbies were pansies.

Fares were theoretically governed by the meters. In all fairness it should be noted that a few meters were reliable, and some of the cabbies were honest. But, for the most part, the bushy beards and dirty lavender and blue and white turbans hid the conscience of burglars.

And not all the cabbies were queer. Frequently they would drive a solitary white or Anglo-Indian female fare to a secluded spot and practice rape as well as robbery.

However, generally, the Drivers managed—as did the jungle-crazy ex-Marauders and Marsmen, who were lucky enough to get a Calcutta furlough—to slap the big, bewhiskered boys down to their proper stature in Calcutta life.

The American military, with typical efficiency, set up an ornate bus system of transportation from the heart of Calcutta—hard by Chowringhee Street—to virtually every Army installation in and out of town. But after the final buses left at midnight, the prowling Sikh cabbie came into his own.

"The meter say three ruPEES, sahhb"—this with white teeth flashing from a black, oily beard. "But you pay ten ruPEES more."

The uninitiated argued—and wound up either walking or else on a ricksha. The smarter lads agreed. But at destination the argument began.

"But sahhb—sahhb. Petrol is rationed, sahhb. Me poor man—"

"Gwan yuh black sunuvabitch!"

"Sahhb—sahhb!"

"Listen, you pansy bastard, scram the hell outta here or I'll jerk that beard of yours out by the roots, hair by hair!"

The thin, wiry ricksha boys—Bengali for the most part—hated the overgrown, bullying Sikhs. And when Americans argued and browbeat the cabbies, the ricksha wallahs crowded around and grinned and jabbered and applauded enthusiastically.

Stories and articles and Renowned World Travelers' Tales always have described those majestic creatures as noble and brave people—but to the average Driver on leave and furlough in Calcutta, the Sikh cabbie was a comic-opera figure with a greasy, infested beard; oily skin; and larceny in heart and glance . . .

#32
A GRAY DAY NEAR KUNMING

A Grey day
near Kunming

A GRAY DAY NEAR KUNMING

THE REAL monsoon was only weeks away, but still the sky was overcast and a thin, raw drizzle made each dawn watery and gray.

Not far from the rambling compound that surrounded the Fourteenth's headquarters stood the one-story home of General Chennault.

In front of the house could always be seen staff cars, jeeps, and Command cars: unmistakable signs of military affluence and prestige. The vehicles were always shiny and neat regardless of how thick the Kunming mud was. And the enlisted drivers and lounging officers were as neat and supercilious as the cars.

Overhead could be heard the constant drone, drone, drone of traffic as airplanes circled back and forth—stacked as high as 18 and 20,000 feet—waiting for traffic to let them down to the Kunming runways.

One C-46 suddenly materialized from the mist. It came low and barely whisked over the Fourteenth compound. Passersby froze on the road; the loungers in the general's courtyard straightened up and stared.

The airplane faltered and nosed directly for the house. It grazed the roof and settled to a sudden, crunching stop. Mud splattered as the wings crumpled and the two engines tore loose and ploughed ahead.

Twisting, writhing figures paced the engines. The figures came to a halt and sprawled like rag dolls tossed into a corner.

Cars stopped and people began streaming toward the crash. There were Americans—officers and enlisted men, Chinese coolies, peasants, soldiers, and civilians.

They came to within five paces of the crumpled airplane and formed a jostling, chattering, shouting circle. The three figures who were spewn from the twisted cockpit were not silent. They writhed, and from out of mouths that were dark holes set against a crimson background came unintelligible sounds that were deep and awful in their stark pain.

Their arms were twisted at odd angles and flopped loosely; the clothing was torn and ragged—their legs feebly kicked or twitched and their backs would arch spasmodically.

They looked like the thousands and thousands of ragged dying and wounded Chinese who covered each silly battlefield from the Hangchow Rice Bowl on down to the Salween and the Burma jungle.

They did not at all resemble American fliers—

Someone said: "Hey—there's somebody groanin' in the ship."

It was the crew chief, pinned beneath drums of 100-octane gas.

Faces, white and dusky, peered down. Eyes—black, brown, blue, and green—stared with fascination, eagerness, horror, disgust, and compassion. Slopie kids looked on and opened their mouths, widened their eyes, and giggled and jabbered excitedly with one another, as do kids throughout the world in the face of disaster to others.

An ambulance roared up, left the road, and lurched crazily as close to the wreckage as the rice paddy furrows beneath the slipping wheels would permit. The medics piled out and slithered forward, clutching first-aid kits and stretchers. There was a chaplain with them. He was a short, obese man with a look about him that made one think of a burgher rising during a hearty dinner to answer the sudden demand of a telephone.

While a young GI emptied morphine syrettes into the figures on the ground, the chaplain bent down to listen to the noise that came from those figures.

And, abruptly, the noise suddenly became speech. A pair of gray eyes—livid with conscious pain—looked up, and the voice said, calmly: "My Form One. Get my Form One."

Then the gray eyes fogged over and words became a dreary, sing-song chant of agony.

A little, wizened Chinese woman, her feet deformed and bound, hobbled up and peered. She looked and then pressed her lips together and swayed her head. "Ay-ee, ay-ee." It was soft, almost a sob.

From her—a starveling, with death's arm around her emaciated shoulders—with the cold, gray damp soaking through the rags that covered her—wetting the heavy load of kindling in the pack on her back—from her came that unexpected sound of sorrowful, compassionate motherhood. Americans and Chinese stirred and shuffled their feet and suddenly felt unnerved.

The medics carried the forms—silent now that the morphine had begun its work—into the ambulance. It slowly, gingerly picked its way back to the road and then sped toward the hospital.

The crowd forgot the figures, the little Chinese woman; it moved closer to the wreck. Already other Drivers, healthy and strong, discussed the accident and its cause.

Overhead, the planes still circled and circled in the gray mist . . .

#33
MAINTENANCE

MAINTENANCE

EVERY PLACE that Americans found themselves flying airplanes in had different climatic conditions. No doubt the Aleutians with their dank, damp cold posed a special brand of misery for flight and ground crews. And the Southwest Pacific provided more than its share of suffering.

But this is about China, Burma, and India—about the Hump Drivers and the mechanics who, despite supply inefficiency and egotistic, self-complacent brass hats, kept the 'planes flying.

In the first place, the average GI mechanic was not an expert in the sense that airline mechanics are. Most of the kids in the ATC were youngsters who had received a hasty course in engine overhaul and repair and who found themselves "shafted" to India.

There were no supplies. At least there were never enough to go around. And for a long time there were not enough men. As a result the average day was more than twelve hours.

Sometimes the kids worked eighteen and twenty-hours straight. And, frequently, when the heat was "on," they would work the clock around.

Now this was not heroic. It was not even war. It was just drudge work either under the broiling pre-monsoon sun or else in the dismal rain and mud of the monsoon itself.

It meant fumbling with tools, working in the smothering oily embrace of blistering-hot metal. It was an endless, soul-deadening routine of damp, mildewed clothing and stomach-burning food; fierce heat; or sticky moisture: it represented months and months on end of deadly monotony—of poor, insect-ridden bashies, and no change from the grind of work, work, and more work.

Those who went to China found the routine identical except that the Yunnan plateau was cold, and they exchanged the dull despair of dehydration for the numbed fingers of freezing hands.

Sometimes the Drivers griped and bedeviled the mechanics. But, generally, the poor mechs understood the Drivers, who were just as miserable in their own way.

And if the heat and cold and poor food and bad living conditions were not enough, there was always a headquarter's "Wheel" who would come around and raise hell and insist on Efficiency.

How these kids ever managed to keep the Commandoes, Liberators, Skymasters, and Skytrains going was a miracle. But they did manage . . .

#34
A NIGHT AT THE HO-TA-FU

A NIGHT AT
THE "HO-TA-FU"
Kunming -44-45

A NIGHT AT THE HO-TA-FU

FOR KUNMING-BASED Drivers there was always a sense of excitement to be gained by a visit to one of the many restaurants that thrived in that rambling, dirty, wicked city.

There were a number of well-known places: the Tennis Club, of course, was an extremely high-priced place with an off-limits notice for enlisted personnel. There was the musty, old-fashioned Hotel Du Commerce, which provided clean linen, fair food, and silverware amidst a musty, almost mid-Victorian atmosphere, which, in the background, had toilets that never flushed.

But the favorite place of all was the Ho-Ta-Fu, a crazy, ramshackle three-story side-street establishment that featured Peking-style cooking.

Once in a while the Drivers could borrow a jeep for an evening. The ride to Kunming was exhilarating—truly. The road was paved and straight and lined with tall shade trees. Usually it was cold, and the wind brought tears and a fine glow to cheeks. The headlights would bring out the plodding, pony-driven carts, which were always packed solidly with men, women, and children, and which were constantly cluttering the road.

Then, abruptly, the jeep would turn left and begin to bounce and rattle over the cobblestone paving of Jing Ballew Street. It would chug through the ancient gate, sweep past lines of rickshas, and enter the jammed main thoroughfare of Kunming proper.

Of course before one went to the Ho-Ta-Fu, it was necessary to stop and exchange money. The Drivers were never sure what the rate of exchange would be from day to day. Sometimes it would hover at 500 Chinese dollars to one American dollar. Frequently it would become treble that. But since the restaurant charges would rise accordingly, it did not make much difference.

Money changing was quite an adventure. As quickly as the jeep stopped, it would be surrounded by kids, soft-spoken money changers, and giggling, twittering prostitutes.

"Changee money, changee money?"

"What's the rate, Charley?"

A shadowy, grinning face and the reek of garlic-laden breath. "Fi hundred."

"Nah. Seven fifty."

The face receded. "Nuh nuh. Fi hundred."

The jeep would start on down the street. Again it would stop.

"Changee money?"

"Seven fifty?"

"Six hundred."

"Roger. It's a deal."

Meanwhile the passengers in the back seat had to watch the kids, because in a land of pilferage the street children of Kunming were masters. Despite the alertness of Drivers, however, the kids could and did strip jeeps of spare tires, rearview mirrors, and, on occasion, articles of baggage.

Armed with vast handfuls of banknotes (which Drivers had flown over the Hump), they would turn down the side street toward the restaurant itself.

Because of unsanitary conditions, the Ho-Ta-Fu, along with practically 98 percent of the other establishments in Kunming, had been placed "Out-of-bounds" by the Medical Corps. Therefore, military personnel found here by the MPs would be suspect and liable to apprehension.

However, the MPs usually looked the other way. The regular messes, run for the army by the Chinese-operated WASC (War Area Service Corps), were just as dirty and hazardous, and, besides, the food was of even poorer quality, served in the most unappetizing manner possible.

For a few Chinese dollars, a little street urchin was hired as "jeep boy." His duty consisted of dozing in the car and, presumably, ensuring against theft of all four tires and, possibly, the engine or, at least, the spark plugs.

The Ho-Ta-Fu's stairways were ancient and creaked dangerously. The railings were rickety and, at certain places, nonexistent. For the climber the net result was a spicy shudder as he mounted and peered down over his shoulder into mysterious, murky depths.

The dining rooms, partitioned by glass doors, were generally filled with Chinese and Americans. And it was noisy—almost a bedlam. Chinese people—those who could afford to dine out—are loud, lusty, and uninhibited. They laugh, shout, mess with their food, belch, pick their noses, spai upon the floor, and get uproariously drunk.

At first, for the novice, it was a little unsettling to sit and listen to hawking, gargling, puking sounds coming from the family table in the opposite corner, but old hands quickly got over this, and the sounds became commonplace and unnoticeable—like the muted idling of an airplane's props in a far-off revetment.

The tables were large and circular, and the Drivers sat on low, oblong wood stools. The waiter, a "Shoharr," usually made his grinning appearance, and, next to him, was a tiny replica—a bright-eyed, cynical kid, who was the "Shohitza" or waiter's helper. In America his equivalent would probably be the busboy.

But at this point, the treat of the evening would begin. Someone who fancied himself an expert would impressively order for the gang:

"Kwanchow!"

The Shoharr nodded and scribbled on his pad.

"What the hell is kwanchow?" asked one Driver.

"Hot wine."

"Candied nuts," continued the gourmet. "Hot spring rolls; Bay State Civil Service; roast duck; rice—sweet and sour pork. Daung, Charley?"

The Shoharr nodded. He repeated the order rapidly, and his pidgin English sounded like a chant. The Shohitza sidled up to one of the Drivers and whispered: "Cigalet, Joe?"

"Scram, ya little bum." The Shohitza skipped out, grinning and clutching the cigaret.

The wait for the food was interesting. It was fun to watch the other diners: here a Chinese group were playing a drinking game that involved a yelling of numbers, manipulation of fingers, and then whooping laughter. Evidently the loser had to do a lot of heavy drinking. At another table, a big, fat, full-chicken American colonel struggled with chopsticks and got most of his food down the front of his blouse while his companion, a bored Red Cross girl, tried not to notice.

But finally the service began. First there was a huge bowl filled with hot water. Instantly dishes, chopsticks, and spoons went into it. "Kills the dysentery," explained the gourmet.

"You hope," said another diner.

And then came the hot, crisp, candied nuts and the little teapots that contained the steaming wine. It was poured into tiny cups.

"Gombay," said the gourmet.

"Nuts," said another Driver. "That means down the hatch. Let's take it easy. Let's sway-bee-yen."

That meant to drink the wine slowly. Some gombayed. Others sway-bee-yenned. The wine was very warm, and it gave everyone a pleasant buzz.

"What is Bay State Civil Service?" asked an initiate.

"Sort of a dish of chopped, cooked cabbage and meat," explained the gourmet. "Damn good, too. The Slopies call it "by sy tuhzilly tzur," but I found out that it was easier to call it "Bay State Civil Service," and since they know what you're talkin' about, what the hell!"

When the food came, it was like an avalanche. There was the rice in huge, steaming bowls. Instantly the diners dipped in and manners were forgotten. The spring rolls, long, crisp, tasty mixtures of meat, cabbage, and other ingredients rolled into a cylinder of flour, followed. And then came the roast duck—carved into convenient chunks. It was served with platters of unleavened, hot pancakes that looked and tasted something like Mexican tortillas.

The gourmet showed how it was done. Taking a pancake, he smeared it with a thick sauce, placed two green onions into the center—sprinkled on some rice and several pieces of duck, rolled it into a tube, and began to chew.

The others followed suit.

"The hell with these goddamn chopsticks," said a Driver. "I'm gonna eat with my hands."

But most of the others were adept at the use of chopsticks. In fact, chopsticks are not at all a bad gadget for eating purposes.

In between mouthfuls, of course, there was more kwanchow. And the toasts decidedly changed from sway-bee-yen to gombay until everyone felt pretty high.

The final course was the soup—a huge, overbrimming tub of it.

"The Chinks believe in usin' the soup last—wash the chow down," said the gourmet.

"S'dam fine idea," said another Driver.

And finally the feast was done with, and everyone sat around, glassy-eyed and with loosened belts. In the back of their minds was the worry that, perhaps, this time they would get amoebic dysentery. But what the hell. It tasted good, and, besides, the stuff was all hot. That is—except the onions. But what the hell—

"Chittie hai," said one Driver.

"That's Indian, yuh fool," said another. He raised his voice. "Hey, shoharr—bring that goddamn check."

The shoharr presented the bill and everyone's eyes bulged:

"Twenty-two thousand bucks," whistled one of the diners.

Money came forth, and the shoharr and shohitza stood by patiently while the Drivers began assembling five-hundred-dollar Chinese banknotes.

Finally the counting was done with, and the party began to carefully navigate back down to the street.

"Wait a minute," said one of them. "I gotta go find a latrine."

The experienced one guided him into the back, on the ground floor. There was a huge kitchen—primitive, stone-lined, with shadowy cooks attending spitted fowl that roasted slowly over open, leaping fires. There was food and garbage heaped on the ground, and weaving, leaping shadows that one instinctively knew were rats. The latrine was a crevice in the opposite wall, and the two Americans waited until a Chinese cook got through and shuffled past them.

But what the hell—the food tasted good, and besides it was hot and heat killed germs—didn't it?

#35
OFFLOADED MARS MULES IN CHINA

OFF-Loading "MARS" Mules
IN CHINA

OFFLOADED MARS MULES IN CHINA

IN THE spring of 1944, the "tactical" situation demanded that reinforcements be rushed into Assam for the opening of the ground drive that eventually culminated in the recapture of Myitkyina and the subsequent reestablishment of the Burma Road.

The Drivers flew two Slopie divisions from Yunnan-yi to Sookerating in Assam. There the starvelings were deloused, given their first honest ration of rice in months, and then reequipped with guns and bullets for the opening of the eastward drive into Burma.

These two Chinese divisions, the 14th and 50th, formed part of what afterward became known as the "new" Chinese army. It was new in that each soldier had gained at least 15 pounds in weight; wore a semi-British-American uniform, and had individually developed a taste and ability for thievery that still can stand as a record in itself, military history to the contrary notwithstanding.

By April of 1945 the air movement was in reverse. The Wheels let it be known that the Noble Chinese's new divisions would fly en masse back to China and then would proceed to make hash out of whatever Japanese remained in and around the theater.

Because the new Chinese army had tried, in Burma, to fight Japs for a change (in between sniping at Americans), an order went out that each Slopie soldier would be rewarded by being permitted to bring his individual loot back with him.

The Drivers found themselves loading troops who carried as many as eight to ten GI blankets, dozens of cartons of cigarets, and several guns per man. These troops were cocky, and occasionally they looked better dressed and nourished than the Drivers themselves!

This definitely did not engender love. But one compensating part of the operation consisted of the airlift of horses and mules.

These animals had originally been part of the Mars Force, a group of two regiments of Yanks who had succeeded the poor, battered, knocked-out Marauders.

The four-legged passengers presented something new to the Drivers. How would horses and mules react to airplane rides? The method of loading was simple. Hard-bitten mechanics of the troop carrier squadrons, assigned to Burma, outfitted C-47's with bamboo-and-wood stall-like partitions.

The horses were loaded forward, and the mules, slightly smaller and lighter, stood directly behind them. Two horses and two mules. In the rear were herded a couple of Chinese hostlers plus several bags of feed.

The Drivers watched the Mars GIs plead, shove, and otherwise pack the dubious four-footed passengers into the ships. Then the Drivers would sidle past the animals and enter their cockpits and turn the props, hoping for the best.

But these silent riders were wonderful customers. They did not stink. They remained quietly at their places. The only thing wrong was offloading. Someone, on the China side, forgot to provide ramps. Several of the animals, yanked by their Chinese hostlers from the 'planes, jumped and injured themselves. Unfortunately the animals had to be shot. Most of the Drivers would rather have shot the hostlers, but the Wheels wouldn't have cared for that.

Actually the move from Burma to Kunming and Chanyi was only Part One. Part Two began shortly afterward, when it seemed as though the Japs were on their way to capturing the air base at Chihkiang, which is about 500 miles airline north and east of the Kunming area.

The Drivers were given a simple assignment: merely to airlift over 20,000 troops, 3,000 horses and mules, and 2,500 tons of equipment from the Kunming area to the threatened airbase. The move was done without the loss of a single man or beast—or even an ounce of supply.

But everyone fell in love with the Mars mules and horses: they were SUCH nice, sweet-smelling, easy-to-get-along-with passengers!

APPENDIX: OTHER WARTIME DRAWINGS BY ARTHUR LA VOVE

APPENDIX

EDITORS' NOTE: For the sake of completeness, we have included three wartime illustrations by Arthur La Vove that are unconnected with his time as a "Hump Driver."

Arthur La Vove, lieutenant colonel, United States Army / Air Force—China-Burma-India theater of operations

"Burying the Dead" (San Pietro, Italy)

"10 Minute Break"

"His First Love!"

Arthur La Vove was a writer, artist, journalist, and pilot who lived and worked during a pivotal time in American aviation and military history. He was born on Manhattan Island in New York City, USA, on December 6, 1909.

He flew his first airplane from Roosevelt Field in Long Island, New York, in 1929. He then went on to fly as a pilot for the first transcontinental airline in American history—Century Airways—and, subsequently, for United Airlines in the late 1930s, while enlisting in the Air National Guard prior to the attack by imperial Japan on Pearl Harbor and America's entry into World War II in December 1941.

He attended Columbia University's School of Journalism in New York, and he was a working police and aviation reporter for both the *Herald Examiner* and the *Los Angeles Times* in Southern California through the 1930s and '40s and up until the mid-1970s. He was an active commercial pilot during the 1930s and '40s, and he witnessed and experienced the beginnings of modern commercial airlines and commercial aircraft manufacturing, particularly on the West Coast in Southern California.

He knew the founders of Pan American Airways, and of Mexicana Airlines—a subsidiary of Pan American. He flew airplanes for William Randolph Hearst and his family to and from San Simeon, and he knew Howard Hughes.

Finally, and no less interestingly, Art La Vove drove in the last Mexican Road Race in 1953 through Baja, California, and he was involved with the expedition to excavate pre-Columbian artifacts in and around Mexico City, Mexico, during the 1930s, most likely piloting an airplane that transported artifacts and personnel.